MW00438726

Glass Plates & Wagon Ruts

Glass Plates & Wagon Ruts

Images of the Southwest by Lisle Updike and William Pennington

H. Jackson Clark

UNIVERSITY PRESS OF COLORADO

Copyright © 1998 by the University Press of Colorado
International Standard Book Number 0-87081-495-8

Published by the University Press of Colorado
P.O. Box 849
Niwot, Colorado 80544

All rights reserved.
Printed in the United States of America.

The University Press of Colorado is a cooperative publishing enterprise supported, in part, by Adams State College, Colorado State University, Fort Lewis College, Mesa State College, Metropolitan State College of Denver, University of Colorado, University of Northern Colorado, University of Southern Colorado, and Western State College of Colorado.

The paper used in this publication meets the minimum requirements of the American National Standard for Information Sciences — Permanence of Paper for Printed Library Materials. ANSI Z39.48-1984

LIBRARY OF CONGRESS CATALOGING-IN-PUBLICATION DATA

Clark, H. Jackson, 1924–
    Glass plates and wagon ruts : images of the Southwest by Lisle
Updike and William Pennington / H. Jackson Clark.
        p. cm.
    ISBN 0-87081-495-8 (cloth : alk. paper)
    1. Photography—Southwest, New—History. 2. Updike, Lisle,
1890–1970. 3. Pennington, William M. 4. Southwest, New—History—
Pictorial works. 5. Four Corners Region—History—Pictorial works.
6. Frontier and pioneer life—Southwest, New—Pictorial works.
I. Updike, Lisle, 1890–1970. II. Pennington, William M. III. Title.
TR23.9.C58 1998
779'.3679—dc21   98-26196
                                                            CIP

07 06 05 04 03 02 01 00 99 98   10 9 8 7 6 5 4 3 2 1

Frontispiece photo, entitled "Relating an Experience," is part of Pennington and Updike's Navajo series.

To Elizabeth Testa,
horsewoman, writer, friend

〜

Contents

Foreword

Journey Into Yesterday

The American Southwest of ninety to one hundred years ago has emerged as a legendary, romantic land and people—a Camelot lost, that can never be regained. As the British poet, Charles Kingsley, wrote "So fleet the works of men: Back to the earth again, ancient and holy things fade like a dream."

Fortunately, that dream has been preserved, at least in black-and-white photos by two little known Durango photographers—Lisle Updike and William Pennington. Just after the turn-of-the-century, they roamed this vast land (the Four Corners states of Utah, Arizona, New Mexico, and Colorado), photographing a variety of landscapes and a multitude of people. They secured "the shadow, ere the substance perish," as Denver newspaperman, William Byers, urged his readers back in 1861. Byers wanted them to have their photographs taken.

The late H. Jackson Clark, third generation Durangoan, Southwestern scholar and writer, a sojourner throughout the land, folklorist, and friend of almost everyone he met, knew both men. This gives the book a personal flavor that cannot be achieved in any other way. Although Updike and Pennington were entirely different personalities, they had a common goal in capturing that "shadow." Fortunately, with his love for the region and understanding of history, Jackson helped to save these photographs, as well as putting together this fine collection for publication, where they are a tribute to a people and their fascinating land. It is only to be regretted that he died before this true "labor of love" saw the light of day.

With his sensitivity for the region and the early decades of the twentieth century covered by these photographs, Jackson has managed to open the readers' eyes to another time and another place. The land might seem hauntingly familiar. Little else is today.

So leave the present behind and come back into history—not long ago really. Welcome back to only yesterday in man's millenniums of struggle to live in the Southwest's Four Corners. Savor the text. It sets the scene. Then, as the reputed Chinese proverb says, "a picture is worth a thousand words." An even more exciting treat is awaiting, as you have the opportunity to go with Updike and Pennington and see what they saw through their cameras. A memorable journey is in store for you without the hardships that they had to face.

—Duane A. Smith

Introduction

In the early years of this century, William Pennington and Lisle Updike roamed the Four Corners area of Colorado, Utah, New Mexico, and Arizona, photographing people and landscapes. They traveled on horseback, by narrow gauge railroad, horse-drawn wagon, or Model T Fords, sometimes working together from the studio they shared in Durango, sometimes working alone. They went to mining camps in the nearby rugged San Juan Mountains as well as to the Navajo, Jicarilla Apache, Acoma, and Zuni Indian reservations.

Pennington and Updike had entirely different personalities and backgrounds but they shared similar goals. Each wanted to be recognized as a fine photographer—specifically, as Updike once said, "the best in the country." The strength of their long relationship lay in their diverse talents as well as in their mostly complementary approach to work and to life in general.

I knew both men. I was born and raised in Durango, Colorado, at a time when William Pennington owned and operated the Pennington Studio. As a youngster I frequented his studio on Main Avenue with his grandson, my good friend Allan Bates. Pennington generously let us come into the darkroom and watch him work. I loved the smell of the darkroom chemicals and the magic of seeing images appear on paper as the chemicals did their work in the developing tray.

I also remember Lisle Updike from my childhood. He was a customer of Jackson Hardware Company, my family's store, on his visits to Durango. He had a long association with my grandfather, Harry Jackson, and seemed to be particularly fond of my mother, Marguerite Clark, whom he always called "Margaret."

In the years after World War II, I saw Lisle frequently at Rotary Club meetings during his summers in Durango. In his later years I helped him liquidate his Indian art collection and I purchased from him many of the glass plates, negatives, and prints that appear in this book. My son, Jackson II, and I tape-recorded several lengthy interviews with him in the early 1970s. Lisle and I were good friends until his death in 1976.

Neither Lisle Updike nor William Pennington achieved the fame of Edward Curtis, William Henry Jackson, Alfred Stieglitz, or A. C. Vroman, but the quality of photographs these two pioneers produced compares favorably with the work of those other master photographers of the period. The body of Pennington's and Updike's work is truly representative of the two men and their time and place in Southwestern history. The following photos, rarely shown anywhere but in the Four Corners area, are now highly valued and eagerly sought by collectors.

Glass Plates &Wagon Ruts

Chapter

1

Lisle Updike, born in 1890 in Erie, Pennsylvania, was the grandson of a boat operator on the Erie Canal.

From his early childhood, Lisle and his parents were almost constantly on the move. Lisle's father was a gypsy at heart; George Franklin Updike loved taking his wife, Myra Mitchell Updike, and his son and daughter on the open road. A lifetime of travel never completely satisfied his longing to explore new places and meet different people.

The Updikes traveled from place to place by train, by riverboat, and by horse and wagon. "Home" was wherever the senior Updike said it was. It might be where they pitched camp for the night, over the next ridge, or across a river. It could change at the drop of a hat. Opportunities were everywhere and each day presented new challenges. The family for the most part accepted the hardships of living on the road as part of life and dealt with them as they arose.

George and Myra Updike were on the road most of the time for more than forty years, traveling from north to south and from east to west, always looking for that special place to "settle down." They would still be on the road, in a place near Kingman, Arizona, in July 1919, when sixty-nine-year-old George dropped dead of a heart attack.

His son, Lisle, would be forever shaped by his father's wanderlust.

George Updike was a first-rate bronco-buster, horse trainer, roustabout, salesman, and part-time Pinkerton detective. He made money whenever and wherever he chose. He was an experienced cook and through the years owned and operated restaurants or cafes, which he then sold when they became profitable. Moving from camp to camp, hotel to hotel, town to town, the family did not stop in one place long enough to establish roots. Lisle Updike never had a real "home town."

In 1900 the Updikes arrived in San Antonio, Texas, after a short stay in New Orleans. By then, the family had been crisscrossing the country for more than a decade (with a side trip to Alaska and Canada thrown in) and had passed through San Antonio several times during that period. For Myra Updike, "the Alamo City" was one of her favorite places, and her husband sensed opportunity in the rapidly growing town.

In the heart of old San Antonio, George found a "perfect building" for a restaurant at 132 Solidad Street, which he always referred to as the "Old Spanish Palace." It was right on the bank of the San Antonio River and lots of potential customers passed by on their way to the Buckhorn Saloon and the stores downtown.

The building had limestone walls two feet thick and a huge courtyard with massive gates to accommodate large wagons. George Updike fixed up the back rooms of the complex for living quarters. In the main building he installed a long lunch counter with more than fifty stools. He advertised the restaurant as "The Boston Short Order and Lunch Room, 132 Solidad Street, Leaders in Low Prices and Good Home Cooking."

Lisle, then ten-years-old and a regular helper in the family enterprises, distributed advertising handbills up and down Houston, Commerce, and Solidad Streets, and as far as Alamo Plaza and the historic Menger Hotel. Handbills were an inexpensive form of advertising, which he would remember later for his own ventures.

At his "Lunch Room," George Updike offered the best food at a cheaper price than the competition. Coffee with cream was five cents, a plain steak was ten cents, and a small Porterhouse steak with potatoes was fifteen cents.

Within a few months business was booming and, as usual, George Updike said it was time to take the profit, sell the business, and move on. On March 24, 1901, he sold the business to a Mr. McKinney, then loaded the Updike family and possessions into a newly purchased "hack," or spring wagon, and left San Antonio. The family embarked on a year-long odyssey that took them to Fredericksburg, Mason, "the lovely little town of Buffalo Gap," Texas, and out into the plains of West Texas. With only a few days' rest at any one place, they moved on to explore the snowy mountains of Colorado and the deserts of New Mexico and Arizona.

The roads were primitive at best and in some cases practically non-existent. The hack broke down twenty miles from San Antonio and the family had to wait several days for repairs. It broke down again in Fredericksburg and yet again in Mason. Myra wrote forlornly in her diary that "I wish we might have settled down in one of the lovely little German towns with so many friendly people." But George Updike always had his eye on some distant horizon and the family was on the road again as soon as the repairs were finished.

It was a year of strenuous travel relieved by visits to old friends and punctuated by long walks across barren deserts and over frozen mountain passes. While George and Lisle found everything fresh and exhilarating, the many hardships of the trip brought illness and despair for Myra and Lisle's sister, Alma. This particular journey for the Updikes ended when Myra Updike finally issued her ultimatum: "I've had enough. I'm tired, I'm worn out, and I will never travel like that again." The Updikes had covered more than three thousand miles since leaving San Antonio twelve months before.

To George, every new day had been an adventure, as he bought and sold items along the way and made money by trading. He called this his lifetime work, and attributed his success to the fact that he was the "fellow from out-of-town." But when Myra said that she would no longer live like a gypsy, George reluctantly agreed never to subject his wife and children to another wagon trip like the last one and promised to search for that elusive place where the family could settle at last into a steadier life. George Updike sold the wagon and team in Wilcox, Arizona.

For Lisle, the trip had been a revelation. He saw people and places he had never imagined, and he loved it all. So when George promised Myra a permanent home (a promise he never actually fulfilled), young Lisle had other ideas. He said, "I liked being on the move and I didn't want to stop traveling. I wanted to have my own hack and be able to go anywhere I wanted. I had acquired the traveling habit and it became a part of my nature. For many years I traveled thousands of miles with a wagon or pack outfit all over the United States. I never thought about settling down."

Lisle had owned his first camera before the age of ten. He early on fancied himself as a "pretty fair photographer." He had also learned to make jewelry from copper wire, which he had ordered from a Chicago mail order house. So, not long after the Updikes arrived in Arizona, Lisle, age twelve and equipped with his cherry wood Hawkeye camera and his jewelry-making skills, felt well prepared to leave the family circle and set out alone.

At first, he would take off for one or two days, and then go for a week or more. Lisle loved his parents, but he was anxious to be his own boss. Large for a twelve-year-old, Lisle had no trouble passing for eighteen. Finally, after several short partings, his family recognized how urgently Lisle wanted his independence and gave him their blessing.

Sometimes the Updikes would not see Lisle for several months, so together they devised a way of staying in touch. They made an agreement to write in care of General Delivery in the capital city of the state where they last had met; from there, the letter could be forwarded. It was a system that worked even when they were thousands of miles apart.

They had another scheme to find each other through *Billboard*, a magazine for show people that listed all the upcoming fairs, carnivals, circuses, wild west shows, Chautauquas, races, and reunions. The magazine ran a list of letters in every issue, such as "Mrs. George Updike has a letter here from Cincinnati." Despite the distances separating them, the family remained close, and whenever their paths came near they always managed a reunion.

Lisle's childhood as a vagabond influenced the shape of his entire life. Wanderlust was not only his inheritance; it also was the foundation for his interest in people and places, an interest which would be so well expressed later in his photographs.

Chapter

2

In 1904, when most boys his age were still in school, fourteen-year-old Lisle Updike bought a ticket on the *Robert E. Lee*, bound for the St. Louis World's Fair, ready with plans to make his mark by taking photos of fair visitors. He convinced himself and his customers that he was an experienced photographer despite his youth. Promising next-day delivery, he would retire to his hotel room (transformed into a darkroom by hanging hotel blankets over the windows) to develop his glass plates. He would then thrust the developed plate, pressed against the light sensitive paper, into the sunlight in the space between the window glass and the blanket, to create the finished exposure. He experimented until he had the delicate timing down pat. However, to his dismay, most customers wanted their photos sooner than he could deliver, and many complained about the unprofessional quality of the prints.

Hoping to gain both experience and access to a more controlled darkroom, Lisle persuaded a fairgrounds photographer to hire him to do the darkroom tasks and let him process some of his own photos on his own time. This was a wise idea on Lisle's part, but he very soon realized it was premature when, after the first day, his boss asked him, "Have you ever milked a cow? If you haven't, you might think about it because you'll do better at that than taking and developing pictures."

Lisle found himself in over his head and insufficiently prepared. Discouraged and angry with himself, he resumed making and selling copper jewelry to earn money. But he did not abandon his photographic ambitions: he studied the art of photography from books and magazines and before long, picked up his camera once again.

Following the *Billboard* event schedule, moving from place to place, Lisle took pictures in the daytime and sold jewelry at night. Ever the true son of the versatile George, Lisle added another skill to his repertoire of money-making schemes: fortune-telling.

Of course Lisle did not know anything at all about predicting someone's future, but he did not let a little matter like that stop him. He knew enough about sales and about human nature to be sure to invent a story that made the customer happy. He acquired a life-size dummy, dressed it in an Arab costume, and mastered a sleight of hand trick to pull a personalized fortune from a pocket in the dummy's garment—the gimmick was always a crowd pleaser. No doubt charmed by hearing a favorable fortune, people bought his jewelry and had a family photo made at the same time. He later said that he "made lots of friends" in those days.

The St. Louis World's Fair was a laboratory and proving ground for his photography and for himself. Lisle recovered quickly from the failure of his first commercial photography effort, and any personal doubts he might have had about his salesmanship quickly vanished in the light of his growing success. Soon he was competing with the best in the business and was well on the way to becoming an accomplished photographer.

After St. Louis, for almost two years Lisle meandered through Louisiana, Mississippi, Alabama, Georgia and Tennessee, outfitted with a camera, a stack of business cards, and abundant self-assurance. He took photos in hotel parlors, at horse trading events, and at county fairs.

After arriving in a new town and renting a hotel room, Lisle would get permission from the hotel manager to use the parlor for a studio. Always the enthusiastic promoter, he blanketed the town with advertising. Tirelessly he knocked on doors, passed out handbills, nailed posters on power poles and buildings, and handed out discount coupons good for family photos to local business owners.

Townsfolk came in droves to watch him fire off flashpowder in his homemade, handheld sheet-metal contraption. The flash seldom failed to entertain the crowd by producing a brilliant light, lots of smoke and fumes, and a fountain of fine white dust. The curious and the timid watched the fireworks from a safe distance, and eager customers waited in line for their turn in front of the camera.

Word-of-mouth brought Lisle as much work as he could handle. By being friendly, charging fair prices, and investing long hours he made money and put much of his earnings into savings. He had begun his life on the road in an economical traveling style, moving around mostly by train and using his hotel room at night as his darkroom, so he soon saved enough to buy two horses and a wagon.

Living was cheap. A good hotel room cost two dollars per night, including meals, while a family photo might sell for fifty cents or three for a dollar. It was not unusual for him to trade a family photo for room and board. Customers who did not have enough money for a photo paid him in trade; in lieu of cash he frequently accepted a ham, a turkey, or a basket of fruit. He then traded these items to a hotel for a room or meals. His father had taught him well.

Years later he recalled, "I wasn't getting rich but I was getting lots of experience and was seeing the country. As long as I could eat regularly and save a little money I was happy."

Along the way, in a southern town he picked up a partner who knew nothing about photography but who had a flair for showmanship akin to his own. The fellow played a guitar, sang folk songs, and became a straight man for Updike's sales pitch. Updike quickly learned to strum the guitar, pick a banjo, and sing along. The itinerant pair developed a routine: after they had set up camp on the edge of town in an open space large enough to accommodate a crowd, Updike would canvass the town with cards and posters. When darkness fell, all would be ready. They would ignite an enormous bonfire and sit back, waiting for the people to come.

And come they did. The crowds flocked to see the fire but stayed to hear the music and the sales pitch. Updike and his cohort dished out all the excitement of an old-time Medicine Show. There was not much for people to do in small southern towns in those days, and the two showmen gave their customers something lively and different.

Updike recalled, "Sometimes we'd work all day developing and printing to get ready for the evening's trade. When business began to slack off, we'd move on to another town, always checking in *Billboard* for profitable events and messages from the folks. Sometimes a customer would recommend a community where we'd do well. We usually had the name of some business person to contact. A free photo or a piece of jewelry usually put us on the right track."

Up to this time Updike's skills had been limited to glass plate photography, but he became fascinated with tin-types, a one-of-a-kind photo made by exposing a metal plate with light sensitive emulsion on it. He experimented with a handmade tin-type camera, but found it was inefficient because the plates had to be developed in a darkroom. To speed up the process he designed and constructed a self-contained camera and photo lab all in one compact wooden box covered with leather. It had a peephole for a lens, a shutter, and hand holes on each side where he could reach in and focus the lens on a piece of ground glass.

When everything was ready, Updike would expose the emulsion-coated metal plate and then drop it into the developing solution in the bottom of the camera box. Then, by careful timing, he would slip the finished tin-type into a washing solution underneath the camera. Presto! After a few minutes the metal was dry and he would hand the finished product to the delighted customer.

Updike was charging two to three dollars for a tin-type that cost him less than twenty-five cents to produce, and he calculated that it cost less than five dollars to make the whole camera. The young entrepreneur was soon making tin-type machines in his spare time and selling them for as much as one hundred dollars each.

The photographer-musician's arrangement prospered until the dark day when Updike realized that his helper preferred whiskey to photography or music. Updike also learned, to his disgust, that the man had been diverting partnership money for his own use to buy booze and to entertain a floozy or two. After an angry confrontation, the fellow slipped away in the middle of the night, taking much of their bankroll with him.

Updike took it in stride. "I didn't let it bother me. I'd developed a good sales pitch. With or without a partner I'd make out. I decided I'd better find a town and settle down for awhile. My folks always liked Texas and Texas people, so I decided I'd move to Dallas."

Determined, confident, and with all the world-wise savvy he had acquired in his time on the road, he opened a studio at 485 Main Street, Dallas, in 1906. Lisle Updike was only sixteen-years-old. And he probably did not realize the new direction his life would soon take when, a short time after opening his studio, he met William Pennington in Dallas on business from McKinney, Texas.

Chapter

3

Born in Kentucky in 1874, William Pennington chose a career in photography at an early age. He acquired his first camera by the age of ten and made an effort to gain experience with any photographer who needed part-time help and didn't mind a youngster hanging around the darkroom.

Magazines of the day romanticized "The West," and Pennington yearned to experience frontier life. He wanted to see the wide open spaces and the towering mountains, the colorful deserts, and especially the dusty towns teeming with cowboys, pioneers, and Indians—all the wonders those magazines promised.

In the late 1890s, still in his early twenties he set out for Texas, stopping briefly in Arkansas to work in a professional photographer's studio. By the time he arrived in McKinney, Texas (a small town north of Dallas) sometime around 1902, he had acquired a wife and the need to support his growing family. Unwilling to risk failure, he opened a studio featuring the most reliable trade items of his day: family portraits, wedding photos, and postcards. The studio may have brought in a steady income, but Pennington was less than thrilled by its safe format and its too civilized location. In 1902 McKinney had a healthy cotton farming economy, with successful banks, full churches, good schools, and even an opera house—a far cry from the rough and romantic "cowboy" West he had envisioned.

Meeting Updike that day in Dallas, Pennington must have been caught up by Updike's adventurous spirit and tales of past travels. Perhaps even vicarious "Western adventure" seemed better to Pennington than none at all, so he agreed to create an informal partnership with the energetic young man. And Pennington's greater technical experience as a photographer must have held an equal attraction for Updike, still young to the craft.

Updike recalled the meeting: "We met one day and got along fine. I was always on the lookout for good photographers and Pennington was a master."

The two men formed a loosely organized association working from three separate locations: Updike's Dallas studio, a branch studio he had opened in Waco, and Pennington's McKinney place. Specializing in family photos and scenic postcards, they established a pattern that nicely matched their skills and temperaments: Pennington did the studio and darkroom work, while Updike stayed outside the studio taking photos of families, businesses, and ranches.

Disappointing for both of them, their promising enterprise was short-lived. By 1907, Pennington had developed tuberculosis. Closing the McKinney studio, he moved to Albuquerque with his wife, Rose, and their five children, joining tuberculosis sufferers from all over the country who were streaming into New Mexico to take advantage of the reputed healing benefits of the high, dry climate and the clean air.

And Updike was exhausted from the demands of running both his Dallas and Waco operations while also sharing a business with Pennington. He had stretched his resources and his energy to the limit, and besides, "business was not that good." Travel was hard and the distances between studios and customers were great. So when his father wrote to urge him to join his family in a move to Durango, Colorado, Updike was ready for the change.

George Updike had heard that the Durango area offered plenty of jobs in the thriving mines, mills, and sawmills. The San Juan Basin, known as "The Silver San Juan," sounded like a place of great opportunity. George knew the country pretty well. He and Myra had been to Durango at least once before, making a brief stop on the long trip from Texas to Arizona.

Lisle Updike relished the challenge of exploring a new territory and agreed to meet up with the family in Pecos, Texas. Making the journey with his father would be a pleasure and he remembered Colorado fondly. He had put in some time as a farm hand in the lovely Arkansas Valley as a child of eight or nine before the family had moved to San Antonio.

Before Updike could take off for Pecos, he had to liquidate the Dallas and Waco studios and salvage what he could from the Pennington partnership. During his short stay in Waco, he had recruited a helper to do the darkroom and other inside tasks. So when the Pecos trip came up, Updike asked the fellow to join him and the two headed west in the helper's wagon. They took their time crossing Texas, stopping in small towns along the way to take pictures, tell fortunes, and sell jewelry and a tin-type or two. The family would wait for him. Time was less important than the possible adventures of the road.

Updike and the helper arrived in Pecos sometime in 1907 and agreed to split their assets. Updike traded his latest model "picture box," which could produce postcards almost as fast as his tin-type machine, for a team of horses and a wagon of his own. He and his father headed north, leaving Myra and the rest of the family in Pecos.

They started for Durango with their wagon, team, and saddle horses, stopping along the way in Santa Fe. Then they moved on to spend several weeks in the Colorado mining camps along the Arkansas River not far from Salida, Colorado. Lisle especially was impressed by the mining camp of St. Elmo. George Updike recalled that he had briefly considered stopping there to open a business when the family had traveled through the Arkansas Valley back in 1901. (Many years later Lisle built a scale model of the town, which is now on display in the Arizona Historical Society Museum in Phoenix.)

Father and son crossed over the same mountain passes they had traveled over with the whole family years before. Once again, Lisle was awed by the mountains and by the formidable beauty of Colorado.

Soon after arriving in the Durango area in the summer of 1907, Lisle, who had just turned seventeen, resumed his photography work. Father and son set up camp on the outskirts of town and Lisle began contacting potential customers, but his progress was abruptly interrupted by a near disaster when George chose to ignore his son's advice to "stay away from the stallion." He was almost killed when Lisle's horse severely bit him in the chest, knocked him down, and trampled him.

George was in terrible shape, with several broken bones that would take many weeks to heal. Lisle just put up a tent where George lay on the ground and began to nurse him back to health. George recovered and, as Lisle said, "didn't mess with my stallion after that." Lisle notified his mother but George was back on his feet before his wife and daughter arrived. The George Updikes remained for only a few months in Durango before moving on again; this time back to Texas.

While his father recuperated, Lisle went from house to house taking photos and selling postcards. Young as Lisle was, his career had already spanned five years, since he had first left his parents when he was twelve. A canny salesman, he used the same methods he had used successfully in the past and quickly built up a large clientele.

People who knew him in those days said that it was hard not to like him. Big and burly with a youthful face, he inspired trust. He was a driver, an ambitious and impatient youth, who knew what he wanted and did not choose to wait for success to come to him. He delivered on his promises.

Lisle liked Durango well enough but almost immediately after his father's recovery, he felt drawn to wander again, always looking for new and unusual subjects to photograph. He rode the Denver and Rio Grande Railroad's narrow gauge train to Chama and went on to nearby Tierra Amarilla, a place he was to visit many times in the future.

When he arrived that first time, a Spanish Fiesta was in full swing and the town was full of Hispanics dressed in elegant old Spanish costumes. Dozens of Apache Indians wearing beaded buckskins and elaborate eagle feather headdresses mingled with the crowds.

Lisle had not been in Tierra Amarilla for more than an hour when, to his astonishment, he ran into none other than William Pennington taking pictures of the festivities. Updike said, "I went over to Tierra Amarilla and there was Pennington! He was taking pictures like I was. I couldn't believe my eyes. I said, 'Gee Whiz, I'm glad to see you. I just came from Durango, a dandy town to make money in. Why don't you come and join up with me?' "

It had only been a few months since they had last seen each other and Lisle could not get over the fact that Pennington looked so healthy. He was showing no signs of tuberculosis, other than being slimmer than he had been in Texas. After leaving Texas, he had opened a photography studio in Albuquerque (at 309 West Railroad Avenue, present day Central

Avenue) in partnership with Benjamin Davis under the name of Pennington and Davis. He was getting out of doors more than he had in Texas and he was traveling just like Lisle did. Updike said that it would be a good idea if he moved to Durango so the two could "team up."

By this time, Updike badly needed help with his thriving business. Pennington said that he would have to think it over; he had no money and asked Updike if he could arrange credit for him. Lisle did not know anything about credit but, eager to bring Pennington to Durango, he went to Nelson Second Hand Store and to Tom Graden at Graden Mercantile and contracted to buy the goods Pennington needed. Lisle Updike, age 17, promised the creditors that he would "stand good for it."

He wrote Pennington to tell him that all the arrangements had been made. "Durango is a fine place to live and work, and there is money to be made. Opportunities are everywhere. All it takes to make money is a good idea, hard work, and a reputation for honesty." To Pennington, the Durango that Updike described sounded like the real West, the West that had eluded him for so many years. He packed up his family, cameras, and darkroom equipment, and headed out.

Chapter

4

Set at the point where the San Juan Mountains meet the New Mexico desert, Durango in the early 1900s was a small, prospering mining town, a hub of commerce for the San Juan Basin, and a central connection point for the Rio Grande Southern and the Denver and Rio Grande railroad lines. There were already several good photographers in town, including Frank Gonner, the Boston Studio, the Balster Company, and W. R. Rowland, but there were ample opportunities in the growing community for Updike and Pennington, as well.

Updike was seventeen and Pennington was thirty-three when they formed their second enterprise, but despite Updike's youth and the difference in their ages, the blend of their diverse talents would make their partnership a professional success.

Updike leased space in the Irwin block of buildings at 973 Main and set up a small studio with living quarters for all of them in the same building. The Pen-Dike Studio was born. Updike said, "Right from the start we were making good money and building a fine business. I never liked to work with lazy people, and Penn wasn't lazy. He worked as hard as I did."

Pennington concentrated on formal portraiture. As in Texas, he usually managed the studio and did the inside photography, developing, and printing. He preferred to approach his work in a series of rational, conservative, and carefully planned steps, but was willing to take a chance on the unknown if possible rewards justified the risk. Pennington advertised his work as "Art Photography."

Updike regarded himself more as a photo-historian who recorded the images of time. He began to emerge as the partner with the new ideas. To their expanding practice, he brought his spirit of adventure, love of exploring the unknown, and curiosity about his fellow humans, all qualities well ingrained in his personality. He made things happen and was known as a leader and an innovator, not a follower. Freed by Pennington from the mundane details of running the studio, Lisle eagerly seized the chance to go back on the road. He was in his element, avoiding more predictable routes to delight in taking photographs where few had ever been taken before.

Eager customers in the timber industries, mines, and mining camps of the nearby mountains snapped up Lisle's photos just as fast as he could process them. He joked later that "those men must have had dozens of lady friends, all of them clamoring for pictures." But the mines and mills were located high in the mountains and mountain passes of the mighty San Juan range, the most demanding in Colorado, and while opportunities for spectacular photographs and lucrative assignments were plenty, getting access to them was another matter.

In order to reach his customers, Updike had to drive over roads and trails meant for pack animals and sturdy freight wagons, not for light-weight farm hacks or delicate buggies. After suffering several wagon breakdowns and being detained for days on end for repairs, the determined and practical Updike decided to order a custom-built rig from Jackson Hardware and Implement Company in Durango.

Harry Jackson, originally from Frederick, Maryland, was a blacksmith by trade. He came to Durango in 1881, when the railroad arrived in town. He had worked his trade with General William Jackson Palmer's construction crew on the Denver and Rio Grande Railroad from Alamosa (in the San Luis Valley) to Durango. Almost immediately after reaching Durango, he opened a blacksmith shop catering to all the rugged trades of the area.

There were several hardware stores in Durango when the railroad arrived, but Harry Jackson believed that their prices were too high. Confident of underselling the competition, Jackson started peddling picks, shovels, cable, chain, and dynamite from his shop.

The hardware company flourished and soon Jackson added a line of farm implements to his wares. The buggy and wagon manufacturing was a natural next step for this ambitious fellow, who had the shop, the buildings, the skilled labor, and, by then, the buying power for the materials. Harry Jackson built a retail-manufacturing empire in the 700 block of Durango's Main Avenue.

Jackson developed a reputation for building tough, long-lasting wagons, ideally designed for use in the mining and timber industries. Jackson crafted each wagon with great care for the quality of materials and attention to workmanship. He bought oak especially from Arkansas for the bed of his wagons. When he could not find a manufactured part acceptable to his high standards, he figured out how to build it himself.

He first experimented with steel axles made by Bettendorf Axle Company of Davenport, Iowa, but when he found that they lacked the strength to hold up to the demanding mountain conditions, he designed and built a steel axle of his own.

He specified custom-fabricated wagon wheels to be made from components ordered from the Fort Smith Rim and Bow Company of Ft. Smith, Arkansas. In his shop he installed a huge hydraulic tire setting machine, an enormously powerful piece of machinery used to bond the steel rims to the wooden wheels by hydraulic pressure rather than heat. It was the only one of its kind in Colorado. The wagon wheels were the strongest in the Southwest, capable of carrying tremendous loads over the most hazardous rock-strewn and rutted roads. The Jackson wagon set the standard of excellence for wagons of the time.

Harry Jackson himself was a short, stocky man with biceps and forearms almost as hard as the iron he forged on his anvil. By the time Updike came to discuss plans for his wagon, Jackson's left wrist bore the scars of the countless tiny fragments of red hot metal that had flown off his anvil and become embedded in his flesh as he hammered iron and steel into tools and hardware. He was no longer working as a blacksmith, but was still actively interested in wagon design.

Joe Hollopeter, a master blacksmith, ran the shop for Harry Jackson and was the chief wagonmaker. Intrigued by the unique requirements Updike's work would impose on a wagon, the two men combined their ideas with Updike's and drew up plans.

Hollopeter put his heart into that wagon. When he felt that something had to be changed, he went right ahead and changed it, sometimes overruling both Jackson and Updike. When it finally rolled out of the shop, Updike knew that his new wagon was perfect.

"I'd initially figured that it would cost about $300.00, but before it was finished I had $700.00 in it. I couldn't have asked for a better hack."

It was a good thing for this young businessman that Harry Jackson had taken a liking to him and agreed to finance the price of the wagon.

The mobile studio and photo lab had ample room for all the necessary supplies, including glass plates, chemicals, processing equipment, cooking utensils, lanterns, bedrolls, and clothing—and several firearms. Its unique design permitted Updike to detach the canvas side panel from the wagon and attach in its place a large tent with a canvas floor and a breezeway. (It resembled the awnings and detachable screen rooms seen on modern RVs and trailers.) This unique feature allowed sunlight to filter through the canvas, providing a perfect natural light for daytime photography. The interior of the wagon itself could be completely darkened for developing and printing. It was an ideal rig to carry a photographer over any rough terrain.

Looking into the future in case his association with Pennington fell apart, Updike had investigated the possibility of going to Kimberley, South Africa, but he kept the thought to himself. The time was shortly after the Boer War, and Britain controlled the lush, rich land that attracted immigrants from around the world. Huge diamond deposits had been discovered near Kimberley and Updike had a few contacts there. The wagon would have been just as useful in South Africa as in Colorado.

But while the idea of going to Africa appealed to his vagabond nature, Lisle was still fascinated with the Southwest, its landscapes, its mining camps and the people in them, and especially its Indians.

Pennington, intrigued by the photos that Updike brought back from the field, decided to take a look for himself. The two men began to travel together. First they made short two- or three-day trips into the mountains northwest of Durango to the mining camps near Hesperus at the base of the La Plata Range. Next they went to Cortez, Colorado, where, just as Updike had previously realized, Pennington began to see the potential in photographing the Indians of the area.

Pennington knew little of the Native American culture, but having taken pictures of the Apaches at Tierra Amarilla, he understood the elements required to create outstanding portraits of these distinctive people. He had seen Navajos and Utes on the streets of Durango, but not in their home setting as they went about their daily lives. Someday, Pennington dreamed, he would find a way to capture the images of these Indians.

It did not take long for folks in the area to recognize the talents of the two photographers. By 1908, Pennington had built a solid reputation and was known as the finest portrait photographer in the San Juan Basin. Updike continued to carry his camera to the mining camps, ranches, and county fairs.

Updike followed the fair schedules closely and made sure to be in Durango for the Colorado/New Mexico Fair in the summer of that year. There he and Pennington photographed Harry Jackson and his family in a new Winton automobile which had recently arrived on a railroad flatcar from the factory in Cleveland, Ohio. (This was Jackson's second Winton and he had acquired the Winton dealership for the San Juan Basin, including southwestern Colorado and northwestern New Mexico.) Updike admired the carbide lamp mounted on the left side of the Winton, and told Jackson if he had a lamp like that one he would be able to travel late at night and not have to stop by dark to set up camp. Before Updike's next trip, the enthusiastic crew at Jackson Hardware and Implement Company had installed a similar lantern on the photographer's wagon.

At that same fair Pennington photographed Updike dressed in full cowboy garb posing with his saddle, tack, and saddle horse. Updike was tall and handsome, a good subject, and liked to be photographed. On the other hand, there are few photographs of William Pennington from the Durango days.

Pennington and Updike were making a name for themselves and their studio, but as the year progressed, the partnership faced two challenges. One was internal. When they had set up the business, in Updike's words they "made one mistake. We had one bank account and one checkbook." After a year or so of sharing the studio with Pennington, Updike was pleased with the quality of Pennington's professional work but had one concern: although the profits were good and getting better, the cash flow was impaired by the excessive amounts drawn out of the account by Pennington. Updike said, "I spoke to him about it several times but he always said that he had a big family and needed more money than I did. It didn't seem fair, but I didn't push the issue." The business was making enough to satisfy both of their needs, even if the money was not exactly being distributed equally, so Updike decided to continue on with Pennington.

The other problem was professional: the two photographers felt they lacked a definitive direction for the Pen-Dike Studio. They were willing to take advantage of almost all the opportunities that came their way, but they needed a focus. They talked about their dilemma at length and asked themselves, "What kind of photographic business are we in? Are we going to be satisfied photographing ranches, miners, children, and families?" The studio needed to claim a specialty which would draw attention to the exceptional work the photographers were capable of producing.

Then, unexpectedly, the break they had been waiting for came their way.

Chapter
5

Late in the summer of 1908 Pennington received a form from the U.S. Government inviting the Pen-Dike firm to bid on a unique photography contract. Intrigued, Pennington contacted Updike, who was off in the mining camps deep in the San Juan Mountains. Updike hurried back to Durango and the partners completed the bid form and filed it with the Government. The contract called for the successful bidder to photograph the ruins at the new national park at Mesa Verde.

In 1888 Mancos rancher, Richard Wetherill, and his brother-in-law, Charles Mason, had stumbled across a spectacular ruin of an ancient cliff dwelling (later to be known as Cliff Palace) while they were searching for stray cattle. That same year, they went on to discover Spruce Tree House and other archaeological sites in Mesa Verde. These were not the first discoveries of ancient ruins in the Mesa Verde area, but they were indeed the most significant. As word spread, Mesa Verde became a focal point for archaeologists, anthropologists, and pot hunters.

The Wetherill brothers, with Scandinavian scholar Baron Gustaf Nordenskiold, excavated a treasure trove of archaeological artifacts. As they prepared to send them on the D&RG railroad from Durango to the East Coast for shipping by sea to Sweden, the word spread about the intended shipment and the citizens of Durango rose up in anger and demanded that the articles be retained in Colorado.

As they had broken no law, Nordenskiold and the Wetherills prevailed and the entire collection was shipped to Europe, where it still is today in the custody of the National Museum of Finland. As a result, however, the Wetherills became the object of the preservationists' wrath and were widely regarded as being no better than common pot hunters.

Mesa Verde was no longer unknown territory. The U.S. Government and prestigious museums across the country began to take an interest in the ruins. Something had to be done to stop the pillaging of precious prehistoric relics. Finally, in 1906, largely as a result of pressure from women's preservation groups, the area was designated as a National Park.

Famed ethnologist Dr. J. Walter Fewkes excavated and supervised the reconstruction of Spruce Tree House in 1907. Then a young archaeologist and future park superintendent,

Jesse Nusbaum, began working with Fewkes on the reconstruction of Balcony House, which would be followed by repairs to Cliff Palace. Anxious to entice visitors to the new park, the National Park Service gambled that publishing photos of the reconstructed Balcony House and Cliff Palace ruins would be the key to launching tourist promotions.

In Durango, Mancos, and Cortez there was great excitement about the future of tourism in the area now that they had a National Park in their midst. In this energized atmosphere, Pennington and Updike enthusiastically bid on the project.

There were no roads or water in the park and conditions were primitive in the extreme. Updike had more experience than Pennington with the requirements of a job such as this one, and he wisely noted on the bid form that he was used to handling horses and pack outfits and that it would be no effort for him to do the job. He thought that this would cinch it for them, and it did.

The contract price was eight hundred dollars, with the government agreeing to furnish the horses, camping equipment, a cook, and a guide. The pair agreed to do the job in the winter so that they would have snow to melt for water.

So early in 1909, Updike and Pennington rode the Rio Grande Southern Railroad from Durango to Mancos, the nearest community to Mesa Verde, where they met the government people with their supplies, got their gear together, and started out.

Mesa Verde was not on any highway, major or minor. There simply were no established roads into the park. The photography team traveled for miles and miles, up to the mesa tops on steep trails treacherous with ice, and down into canyons so deep the winter sun never touched the bottom. They went clear to the south end of Mesa Verde to photograph Spruce Tree House. The Wetherills had built a cabin there in the early days and the group stayed in it for a short time, getting a sense of the area and the proper way to portray the essence of these ghostly ruins in their photographs.

Then, after preliminary investigation of the other major ruins, Cliff Palace and Balcony House, the photographers received the frustrating news that they would have to wait for stabilization and reconstruction to be completed before they would be allowed even to begin their photographic work.

Disappointed but assured that their contract would still be honored, Pennington and Updike accepted the delay as part of the job and used the opportunity to view the canyons and explore some of the smaller, less famous ruins.

It may have seemed to Pennington and Updike that they would have no choice but to settle back into their old routine until they could begin their Mesa Verde documentation, but in fact the time at the ruins had nurtured in each man the seed of an idea about the future of Pen-Dike Studio. After returning to Durango from that first trip to Mesa Verde, the two men began discussing similar opportunities.

Updike recalled his childhood visit to the Pueblo of Zuni and recounted the story of it to Pennington. "I told Penn there were people actually living today like the Cliff Dwellers had lived centuries before. I'd been there, I'd seen them. I remember it well." Updike's stories of Zuni appealed to Pennington's imagination, promising him further exposure to that "real West" he constantly yearned for. And the prospect of photographing Zuni was more exciting to him than the assignment at Mesa Verde, a park honoring a dead civilization—after all, real, live people could be found in Zuni.

Suddenly the possibilities for the Pen-Dike partnership seemed limitless.

Early Works

8 PLATES

Updike: First wagon (1904 or 1905). Updike was fourteen or fifteen-years-old.

Updike: Pen-Dike Studio photo wagon built to Lisle Updike's specifications by Jackson Hardware and Implement Company, Durango, Colorado, with steel axles and steel hubs for extra strength on mountain roads.

Updike: West San Francisco Street in Santa Fe, 1906. Lisle Updike and his father stopped in Santa Fe on their way from Pecos, Texas, to Durango.

Pennington: Jackson Hardware and Implement Company, photographed in 1907 (left) and again in 1928 (below), after addition of new storefront. The Blacksmith Shop adjoining had been sold to Joe Hollopeter and Theo Geoglein.

Pennington or Updike, 1908: Harry Jackson and his family in the new Winton automobile.

Pennington, 1908: Lisle Updike wearing his finest cowboy clothes.

Pennington, 1908: Lisle Updike.

Updike Travels, 1910

5 PLATES

Tierra Amarilla, New Mexico, about 1910. Hispanic family wedding photo.

Tierra Amarilla, New Mexico, about 1910. Burro pack train. The Amador Mercantile was adjacent to the T. D. Burns Hacienda, headquarters for the Tierra Amarilla Land Grant. The sign on the Mercantile says, "Aqui Esta Mas Barato," meaning "here is the cheapest place to buy."

About 1910. Two cowboys from the Burns Ranch in Tierra Amarilla.

Salt Lake City, 1910. Salt Air Resort, destroyed by fire several years after Updike visited.

About 1910. Junction Creek and the La Plata Mountain, near Durango.

Mesa Verde, 1911

7 PLATES

Updike: "Penn made this picture. I think it is the best I have ever seen of Cliff Palace."

Balcony House. Once in the ruins, they had to climb, crawl, and squirm their way through tiny doorways and narrow ledges.

Kiva in Balcony House.

Updike and camera perched high on a rocky slope overlooking Balcony House.

Close-up of Updike and camera.

Pennington in main Balcony House plaza, taken by Updike from perch in the rocks. Snow remains on the ledge.

Updike above the main Kiva in Balcony House.

Honeymoon, 1913

22 PLATES

Photo wagon stopped, with a view of the San Miguel Range near Telluride, Colorado.

Jenny Updike is driving on the road high above the San Miguel River near Telluride.

"All the comforts of home" in the Updikes's camp.

San Juan Mountains scenery.

San Juan Mountains scenery.

San Juan Mountains scenery.

Bear Creek Canyon near Ouray, Colorado.

The photo wagon at the bridge over Bear Creek Falls near Ouray. Otto Mears, pioneer road and railroad builder, had erected a toll booth at this spot in the 1880s to collect fees from travelers using the road he had built. By 1913 tolls were no longer collected.

Another view of the photo wagon at the bridge over Bear Creek Falls.

Bear Creek Falls. The abandoned toll booth is in the background.

Photo wagon stopped behind a heavy freight wagon near Bear Creek Falls, on the way to the summit of Red Mountain Pass.

On the way to the summit of Red Mountain Pass.

Updike's famous depth of field technique demonstrated by photos taken on his honeymoon.

Updike's depth of field technique.

Updike's depth of field technique.

Updike's depth of field technique.

Updike's depth of field technique.

Updike's depth of field technique.

Updike's depth of field technique.

Scene by the river, Santa Fe, 1913. Jenny is standing by a large cottonwood tree.

Miscellaneous

5 PLATES

Updike, October 1914. Prominent politicians crowd around Wright B Biplane for a rare chance at a publicity photo prior to an election. Eugene "Bill" Hath, pilot for Berger Aviation Company, flew the plane at the Colorado/New Mexico Fair in Durango.

Petrified Forest 1914. Jenny is standing on a trunk of a petrified tree. The mail truck ran daily between St. Johns and Holbrook, Arizona. Updike: "Jenny climbed up on the tree and a fellow who was riding the mail truck, a Mexican horse thief by the name of Schultz, came and stood near her. I'm standing to the side of the truck."

Will and Sarah Walker Evans, 1925.

Bill MacClary, Will Evans, and William Pennington at the "Window," near either Sanostee or southeast of Ft. Defiance, 1926.

Moving Mountain, Durango, about 1934. Pennington photo.

Chapter
6

Myra Updike's journal tells about the family's earlier visit to Zuni:

November 20, 1902 . . . Packed and left Gallup after dinner. Drove five miles, camped at a ranch under the rocks, well sheltered with a big fire.

December 2 . . . We had a very hard road all day, deep sand and rocky. Came to an old miner's house in the canyon so we could cook in the stove. It's very cold and high here, 7000 feet. George built a fire in the oven. I made biscuits and opened the oven to bake them. It was full of sticks of dynamite. I called George and he got them out, and I baked the biscuits.

December 3 . . . We camped in a canyon by Vanderwagen's trading post. We hear the Zuni will have a ten-day dance soon and we want to be there. Snow is all around us.

December 4 . . . Very cold, drove ten miles through sand. Lots more walking. In Zuni town about 3:00 P.M. A company of soldiers and officers and their wives rode into town. We are glad the Cavalry is here as Zuni has 2,000 Indians and hundreds more coming to the dances. George found a small adobe house for our use. We had to do a lot of cleaning. Talk about Indians, they are thick. We have a nice fireplace and it's truly comfortable.

December 7 . . . Lisle gave me a Zuni silver bracelet today. This is the day with the mudhead dancers . . .

December 8 . . . Lisle gone all day with cavalry officers and their wives to a high mesa where the Indians have had their burial ground for hundreds of years.

Pennington's enthusiasm grew with each story Updike told about the Pueblo of Zuni. He had seen pictures of Zuni taken by earlier photographers and grew anxious to record the faces and ways of these people himself.

Neither of the men knew anything about the terrain between Farmington and Gallup, the closest town to the Zuni Pueblo, and there were no established roads or trails for them to follow. Mr. Allen, who owned a livery stable and a hotel in Farmington, told them about a character named Jim Slade, a freighter from the Red Mesa area of Colorado, who, according to Allen, routinely went deep into the Navajo country to deliver merchandise to the isolated trading posts.

Updike found Slade near a wholesale warehouse in Farmington and told him of their plans. He offered to pay Slade to be a guide, but Slade looked Updike up and down, refused to discuss the job, and quickly walked away.

"I knew," said Updike, "he was afraid of me. I hadn't done anything to threaten him. I just got off my horse and walked up to him and asked him if he'd show us the way to Gallup. Slade was just a little fellow and I towered over him. Maybe my approach was too brusque, but he took one look at my six-gun and rifle in the saddle scabbard and said he didn't have any time for the trip."

Determined to get to Zuni by any means but preferably with a guide, Updike rode back to Durango and told Pennington that he should be the one to talk to Slade. Updike was right: his partner was more tactful. Slade reluctantly agreed to go with them. He liked Pennington but he kept a sharp eye on Updike.

So early in May 1909, William Pennington and Lisle Updike hitched their four-horse team up to their heavy freight wagon loaded with cameras, film, food, and grain for the horses, and made their way south to Farmington where they joined up with Slade. Slade's wife and a Mr. Holgate rode in Slade's wagon with him. (The photographers left the Jackson photo wagon in Durango because they needed to pack more supplies than it could carry on a long trip.)

Following Slade's instructions, the two outfits headed up-river toward Bloomfield, New Mexico, where they planned to cross the San Juan River.

Updike tells about the less than promising start of the journey:

Slade said that he'd ordinarily cross downstream near Kirtland but that the river was in flood stage from the spring runoff, so he wanted to cross a regular ford near Bloomfield. It was all right with Penn and me but it seemed like we were heading in the wrong direction. Our outfit made better time than his did and I wondered why he didn't move along faster. I said, "Mr. Slade, you must have a heavy load there. You're sinking into sand deeper than we are, and we have a heavy cargo." He answered, "I ain't got nothing in there. It's just an empty wagon."

Slade let on that he knew more about the route than he actually did. He couldn't find a good crossing point over the San Juan and we wasted a lot of time. When he finally drove his team into the river his horses were straining and stumbling, and Slade just kept whipping and cursing them. When we got everything across the river, his horses couldn't pull his wagon up the bank on the south side.

Penn and I got our team and saddle horses hitched up with his outfit so we could pull the wagon up the steep bank. Slade took to whipping our horses and I reached up and pulled him down off the wagon and told him we didn't whip our horses, and I wouldn't put up with him doing it. I climbed up in the seat and finally got the rig up the bank.

At this point Updike demanded to know what Slade was hauling in the wagon that made it "so confounded heavy." Slade at last owned up to carrying over two tons of flour for a trading post down the way.

Disgusted with Slade's attitude, the photographers decided to stick with him for a day or so and then they planned to pay him off and go on alone. By this time the two photographers had seen enough to realize that if they kept Slade as their guide they might be weeks getting to Gallup. But the tables turned. Slade begged them not to leave him and his wife and Mr. Holgate. Pennington and Updike took pity on them. They would somehow lead Slade and his companions to their destination, but Pennington would be in charge.

In the end the photographers did not pay Slade nearly as much as they had agreed to, but in Updike's words, "probably a lot more than he'd been worth."

They had already been out for four days, and it was a hard trip the rest of the way, six days or more. They moved steadily each day, carefully eyeing the unfamiliar terrain.

Pennington described the area as the loneliest place he had ever seen. The vast desert south of the San Juan River seemed unending. They passed by an occasional Navajo herder or an isolated hogan, but saw no other signs of human existence until they reached trader Dick Simpson's Gallegos Canyon Trading Post where they camped for the night and bought hay for their horses. From there they proceeded west over land Updike said "looked like the Sahara Desert." They crossed the Chaco Wash, passing north of the ruins at Chaco Canyon.

From the first day they were overwhelmed by the desert. They had never seen anything like it. Even in West Texas they had never seen land so empty of people and animals.

The trip was a constant search for grass and water. They had ten animals to provide for: a four-horse team, two saddle horses, and Slade's own four-horse outfit. Because of an extremely dry spring the grass had not begun to grow, so the need for horse fodder became acute.

Updike remarked in later years, "I knew pretty much what to expect, but Penn had never seen country like this." Nevertheless both of them were surprised to see the miles and miles of exposed seams of coal. They crossed outcrops of coal time and time again. Pennington said, "There must be more coal buried under this desert than there is in the entire state of Kentucky."

The immense bare landscape stretched as far as the eye could see and they sometimes felt as though they were being swallowed up by it. They were awed by the distances, the isolation, and the silence. As Updike said, "I think a fellow could be lonely out there with fifty men alongside him. We knew there were Navajos watching us but we never actually talked to any of them. We'd see them from time to time, watching from high on a mesa or from outcroppings of rock. They were as motionless and silent as the rocks themselves, just looking down and watching us." Several had rifles but the photographers never felt themselves to be in danger.

The wagon ruts which fanned out in every direction were a maze, a puzzle the men had to solve several times every day. When they became lost or confused by the crisscrossing trails, they would try to find a main route. Pennington and Updike would each mount his saddle horse, taking along a rifle and ammunition, and ride out to scout a route to follow. If the trail ended at a Navajo hogan or dead-ended at a corral or an arroyo they would fire one shot into the air. If it appeared to head the right direction, they would fire two shots and then regroup at the point where they had left the wagon.

Using the Lukachukai and Chuska Mountains as landmarks and observing the daily path of the sun and the pattern of the stars in the brilliant desert nights, they traveled southwest until they reached the trading post at Naschitti, forty miles north of Gallup. Naschitti is the Navajo word for badger, so the location was called Badger or Badger Springs.

After a stop at Naschitti, they headed on to Gallup, New Mexico, where once more, Pennington and Updike restocked their food supply. Better aware now of the desert conditions, they also bought hay for the horses. The Slades and Mr. Holgate had reached their destination, a trading post owned by C. N. Cotten, a partner of the famed trader, Don Lorenzo Hubbell. Relieved to be on their own again, Updike and Pennington continued south.

Chapter

7

Zuni Pueblo was an off-the-beaten-track kind of place where Indian traditions flourished. Zuni life in 1909 was much the same as it had been hundreds of years earlier.

Fray Marcos de Niza had come to Zuni in 1538, on a quest to find the Seven Cities of Cibola, fabled places rumored to be so rich that they would put Montezuma's empire to shame. He was followed in 1540 by Francisco Vasquez de Coronado on an equally ill-fated pursuit of the same treasure. Both Spaniards had sought cities with walls of gold but found only rock and adobe villages—no treasure. Much of the original Zuni village had been destroyed by Coronado's frustrated men in their search for Cibola.

Late on a cold afternoon in May, Lisle Updike and William Pennington arrived at Zuni, unannounced and uninvited. While Coronado and de Niza had come to plunder, the photographers came to learn; they came to see for themselves what life was like in a living Pueblo. They hoped to be able to document their discoveries.

The setting sun gave the pueblo walls a golden cast which gradually faded to a muddy brown as the sun dropped below the horizon. Updike had relived his childhood visit to Zuni in relating his memories to his partner, but the Pueblo he found on this chilly spring evening seemed different to him. The buildings were not nearly so imposing, and the place looked as if it had been reduced in scale. During Lisle's earlier visit, the village had been teeming with Indians from distant Pueblos, everyone bustling around with preparations for ceremonies and dances; now it was silent. Smoke from a hundred fireplaces drifted down the river valley. The sky was clouding over, becoming dark with the menace of an approaching storm.

Pennington parked the wagon a respectable distance, perhaps a quarter of a mile away from the pueblo, and Updike headed toward the village to ask permission to camp near the stream. They needed a place to rest with water and grass for their six horses.

Updike probably looked like a giant to the smaller Zunis, some of whom were watching him stride toward the village. He walked with the confidence of a gunfighter, but he must have wondered what he was getting into. He passed close by the cultivated square that made up the Zuni garden plots and across a rickety bridge, all the while keeping a sharp eye on the gathering crowd of people at the entrance to the Pueblo.

Pennington watched this drama play out from his seat on the wagon. He had seen Updike in action before and he knew that Lisle could handle almost any situation. Yet this was the same Pueblo whose citizens had tossed the Fray Marcos de Niza's Moorish slave, Esteban, off the rim of a mesa to prove that he was an ordinary mortal and not a deity.

"I just walked up to the Zuni Indians who were gathering around the houses near the bridge," recalled Updike many years later, "And said we were photographers from Durango, Colorado, and we'd like to get permission to camp and park our hack down by the stream and to feed our horses. In the morning we'd have a look around and maybe take some pictures."

A runner was sent to the home of the man who could determine the photographers' reception. After some time, word came back: permission to stay was granted.

It was dark when Updike returned to the wagon where Pennington waited. They prepared a camp for the night, watered and fed the horses, and cooked their dinner on an open fire. Then they bedded down for the night—with a rifle between their bedrolls.

The day had been calm, clear, and cold, like most spring days in the desert, but as they prepared for the night the clouds became denser and snow showers descended like a gray curtain, obscuring Corn Mesa and other landmarks. The winds came up and the snowstorm blew in. The temperature dropped twenty degrees in twenty minutes. "It was like a Texas Blue Norther," Lisle later recalled. The snow stopped during the night but traces of it can be seen in the photographs taken of the square Zuni garden plots.

After breakfast the next morning, they hitched up the horses, packed their belongings, and drove up to the Pueblo. They received a quiet but friendly welcome. Some parents hustled their children out of sight and away from the camera when the first photographs were taken, but most of the residents welcomed them with smiles and a cheerful wave.

For the next three days the two men made friends, exchanged gifts, and took photographs of Zuni people going about their daily work. Updike amused the Zunis with magic tricks he had learned while traveling in the South. Trust gradually replaced the few suspicions shown the first day.

One of the tribal elders cautioned them about taking photographs of the children. "You might steal their souls," he said. But on the last day of their visit, Updike was allowed to photograph the son of a man known as the chief or headman in the Pueblo. Assured that the strange bulky camera could not indeed steal his child's soul, the father reluctantly gave his permission. One other parent consented to having a picture taken if the child's mother could hold the infant.

Pennington and Updike roamed freely all over the Pueblo taking photographs as they pleased. They took pictures of almost every aspect of Zuni life except a ceremony, including Zuni men drilling turquoise with pump drills, women grinding corn into flour, a weaver, and women carrying water to their garden plots in large pottery ollas balanced on their head. Updike promised to return as soon as possible with the finished photographs.

Zuni was such an exhilarating experience that the two men decided to visit Laguna and Acoma Pueblos on their way home. Two days later they arrived at the base of "The Sky City," the legendary Acoma Pueblo where the natives had lived for centuries on the mesa top formed by hundred-foot-high sandstone cliffs. They received permission to enter the Pueblo and to set up their cameras. No road led to the village so the photographers had to carry their heavy equipment on their backs with additional help from Acoma youngsters eager to make a little money. A trail twisted up a steep path to the mesa top. Again, as in Zuni, their welcome was cordial.

William Henry Jackson and other early photographers had been to Acoma several years before. The old Spanish Mission Church, San Estevan del Rey, dominated the skyline as it had since the early 1600s when Juan Ramirez, a Franciscan, taught the people to make bricks from adobe. Pennington and Updike photographed it from the same vantage point as Jackson had in 1900.

Between Jackson's visit in 1900 and Pennington and Updike's arrival in 1909, restoration had been started on the mission. The Updike/Pennington photographs show that newly made adobes that were being used to reinforce the bell towers and that a few dilapidated buildings in the ancient convento, or priests' quarters, had been demolished.

The visit to Acoma lasted two days. The photographers were eager to return to Durango to develop and print the images they had taken. They headed north toward Durango, pausing briefly at the Pueblo of Laguna, then skirted the eastern slopes of Mt. Taylor and headed out into the vast open land toward the Chaco area and on to Durango.

Back in the studio, they rushed to develop the glass plates and print the photographs. The results were even more dramatic than they had expected. Proud of the photographs he would be able to present to the Zunis, Updike wasted no time loading up his camera, glass plates, other supplies, and the finished prints, and headed south once again. Because he now knew the route and would be traveling alone, he decided to take the Jackson photo wagon rather than the slow and cumbersome freight wagon. He started back to Zuni, confident that he would now have all the work he could handle.

He was to be greatly disappointed. At Zuni he met a group of angry men who said that the youngster he had photographed had died suddenly from a high fever only a few days after Updike had taken his photograph.

A leader of the group spoke angrily, "The boy is dead, and you killed him. You stole his soul. You are not welcome here anymore."

Updike asked to see the boy's father, but he was in seclusion and refused to see the photographer. An antagonistic crowd confronted him and ordered him to leave and not return.

Shocked and saddened by the news and alarmed by the hostility of the people, Updike returned to Durango "almost without stopping." He was too upset to eat or sleep.

Chapter

8

The death of the child affected Updike deeply. He knew that he was not responsible but he had no way to make amends with the father or with the Zuni people. He destroyed the print and the glass plate and never returned to Zuni.

Richard Vanderwagen, lifetime trader at Zuni, confirmed the story of the dead child. "When I was growing up at Zuni during the 1920s, people still talked about the photographer who had stolen the soul of the son of the chief. They didn't forgive or forget."

Pennington, also shaken by the news of the death, lashed out at Updike. He blamed Updike. He rarely said it bluntly but "there were always remarks about my aggressiveness and references to my being too pushy in certain situations. He said, 'If you hadn't insisted, it might not have happened.' He knew that I was not to blame. He was right there with me when I took the picture. I was as upset as he was, but I couldn't do anything about it." During the many years they worked together, this was as close to an outright argument as they would ever come.

Pennington's accusations strained their friendship and exposed feelings of mutual distrust and professional jealousy each had harbored silently for a long time. Pennington could be moody and Updike could be thoughtless. Sometimes it was difficult for them to cooperate in their work together.

While Pennington preached on about Updike's aggressiveness, Updike was resenting Pennington's "free ways with the dollar." He thought that his married partner lavished too much money on his children at a time when the business was barely holding its own and that Penn was not properly controlling his wife's expenditures.

Suspicion and bitterness entered into the relationship. "I started checking the books more carefully," Updike grudgingly recalled. "I wanted to be sure that he wasn't giving away money that rightfully belonged to me." Pennington, the family man, was indeed withdrawing more money than Updike was.

At the same time, Pennington was becoming more critical of Updike's photography. He accused Lisle of not planning his shots well, of tending to "shoot from the hip," as he often would say.

They seriously considered breaking up the partnership and going their separate ways, but the contract with Mesa Verde was still pending. For the time being, the expectation of photographing Mesa Verde would be the bond that kept them together.

Updike had suspected for some time that his association with Pennington might not last, but he wanted to give it every possible chance. As Lisle later said about Pennington, "He was a fine man and I really liked him. . . . I knew that once we got back to working in Mesa Verde everything would be better."

Waiting for notification from the Park Service to resume the Mesa Verde contract, Lisle set off on the road, relieved to be traveling, while Pennington was likewise happy to have Updike away from Durango.

Lisle began going to the Ute Indian Agency in Ignacio, Colorado, where he met Emmett Wirt, a merchant and trader from the Jicarilla Apache Reservation, fifty miles east of Ignacio. The Jicarillas had been shunted from place to place and finally forced by the U.S. government onto a reservation in a remote part of northern New Mexico. By 1910 they had become an impoverished tribe. According to Updike, "Wirt was almost as poor as the Apaches but he didn't know it. Compared to them, he thought that he was well-off."

Always eager to expand his contacts and meet people who might be useful to his career, Updike learned from Wirt that he would be welcome on the Jicarilla Apache Reservation. Wirt provided the introductions and smoothed the way for Lisle to attend the 1910 Jicarilla Apache Fair, where he photographed individual tribal members and family groups.

"They were so poor," said Updike later, "that I told them if they'd allow me to take their photos I'd not charge them anything and they could get a print free of charge when I made the next trip. They went to their homes and came back in wonderful native dress."

From the Jicarilla headquarters at Dulce, Updike continued on to make a return visit to Tierra Amarilla. In years past Tierra Amarilla had been the headquarters for both the Ute and the Jicarilla Apache Agencies, before the Utes were sent off to reservations in Colorado and Utah and the Apaches moved to Dulce.

In 1910 Tierra Amarilla was a small Hispanic town, the county seat of Rio Arriba County and the headquarters for the Tierra Amarilla Land Grant, a multi-hundred thousand acre piece of land that straddled the Rio Chama and spread over the top of Cumbres Pass. The land grant was owned by T. D. Burns and his extended family.

Updike and Pennington had met Burns in Durango, where the New Mexican had founded the Burns Bank. In addition to his ranching, mercantile, and banking empire, Burns was one of the most powerful politicians in New Mexico.

New Mexico, a U.S. Territory at the time, was waiting for statehood. Influential people in the Territory and in Washington, D.C. wanted Arizona and New Mexico combined into a single state. But Burns, a power broker from the old school and a close friend of Miguel A. Otero, Territorial Governor of New Mexico at the turn of the century, believed that both he and Otero would benefit from New Mexico and Arizona being separate states. (In 1912 Burns and his cronies prevailed.)

Updike spent several nights camping on land that would soon be the site for the new Rio Arriba County Courthouse. He photographed a string of pack burros in front of the Burns' hacienda on Tierra Amarilla's main street. Later, before leaving for Santa Fe, he photographed an Hispanic couple following their wedding ceremony, posed with their family by the adobe wall of a local church.

The photographs Updike produced during this period show that he was truly in his element on this trip.

Chapter

9

It was time at last to photograph Mesa Verde. In the late winter of 1911 Updike and Pennington once again traveled to the new National Park, this time to complete their government contract. The ruins of Cliff Palace and Balcony House had been stabilized and were ready for documentation.

Pennington was enthralled by Cliff Palace and photographed it from many different vantage points. But, as he was to discover, the best was yet to come.

An enormous cliff overhang shields Balcony House from view from the canyon rim; this same overhang makes access to the ruin quite a challenge even today. Here was the site of their principal photography assignment, yet the two men could see no easy way to get themselves and their equipment down to it. Apparently all traces of Nusbaum's and Fewkes's paths had been obliterated after the stabilization had been completed. The Park Service intended that all visitors arrive at Balcony House only by way of the ancient paths of the Anasazi.

The government guide led Updike and Pennington along a narrow trail and down an ancient notched tree trunk ladder, the only access to the ruin. From the bottom of the ladder, the photographers and guide cautiously inched their way down to the ruin itself using the hand and toe holds the cliff-dwellers had carved out of the vertical rock face centuries before.

But the Ancient Ones did not have bulky cameras and tripods, heavy boxes of glass plates, and other awkward paraphernalia to cope with. Their large cameras were too ungainly to carry on the delicate climb into the ruin, so the photographers arranged for the cameras to be lowered one at a time in a rope sling from the cliff's edge down to the ruin, one at a time so that if they lost one down in the canyon they would still have another. Retrieving the cameras from the ledge of the ruin proved to be the trickiest part of the operation. Because of the overhang, the bundles dangled just beyond the photographers' reach, so the men had to use a long pole to poke and prod each suspended package until they had maneuvered it close enough to grab and drag onto the ledge.

The photographers carried the glass plates and the rest of their specialized equipment down on their own backs, and the expedition cook stayed above to lower the remaining gear to the waiting group. Once in the ruins, the photographers had to climb, crawl, and squirm their way through tiny doorways and over narrow ledges. Updike questioned whether Pennington would like all the climbing, but "he stayed right with me, never complaining. We were in it together and he enjoyed every minute of it." Apparently the two men were able to set aside their squabbles in a shared love of their subject.

The extra effort required by the site was worth it. The Updike and Pennington pictures rank among the finest early photographs of Mesa Verde. Updike particularly liked the shot he took of Pennington standing in the main plaza of Balcony House with fresh snow on the ledge.

They spent a week in Mesa Verde camping on the canyon's rim. The National Park Service compensated them for their lost time and enthusiastically accepted the photographs.

Unfortunately, even after the great success of their efforts together at Mesa Verde, Pennington and Updike continued to be irritated with each other. Amicable as it had been, the trip to the cliff dwellings had changed none of their basic differences. It was becoming more and more clear to Updike that his partnership with Penn eventually would end, but he wanted to take some time to map out his future. He was not sure how long he would remain based in Durango, but for now decided to concentrate on photographing Native Americans.

He resumed his trips to the Ute Agency in Ignacio. There he photographed Buckskin Charley, the future Chief of the Utes. Updike had first met Buckskin Charley in Tierra Amarilla, New Mexico, at the time he had renewed his relationship with Pennington. Now, years later, Updike and Buckskin Charley became good friends. Buckskin Charley loved to have his photograph taken and over the course of the chief's life, Updike obliged by taking many pictures of him and his wife.

Supposedly, Buckskin Charley spoke little English, but Updike had no trouble communicating with him. They remained friends until the old chief's death in 1936.

Updike relished northern New Mexico and during this period made the trek to Santa Fe many times, sometimes by narrow gauge railroad, but mostly in the Jackson wagon, which as "ideal" as Updike considered it, still had its limitations. Updike had driven it for many years and had covered thousands of miles, but it did break down occasionally. And in addition to repairing wagon parts, Updike had to become skilled at shoeing horses, mending harness leather, and being a veterinarian for his team.

As the year wore on, Updike grew increasingly concerned about the finances of Pen-Dike Studio. Pennington was beginning to be hounded by merchants to whom he owed substantial sums of money. He had continued to draw more money than Updike considered fair and was getting deeper into debt. Updike knew that if he did not leave the partnership he might be forced to pay Pennington's bills.

Although Updike used the money as an excuse, it is probably more true that he resented Pennington's continued reminders about the death of the Zuni child. Pennington was trapped in an unsatisfactory marriage, had a family to care for, and still faced the lingering specter of tuberculosis, and he lashed out at Updike in envy of the younger man's mobility.

By now each of the partners had developed a distinctive camera style of his own. Pennington preferred the posed photo with an emphasis on detail and the focus on a person. Updike wanted to create photographs that reflected his own vision of the West—past, present, and imagined. He liked shots of the wide open spaces and was a master of scenery photos. It no longer seemed appropriate for photographers with two such divergent styles to be in business together. Although Lisle was the first to mention the idea of splitting up, both men recognized that the dissolution of Pen-Dike Studio was inevitable. So after Christmas 1911, Pennington made arrangements to buy out Updike's interest, and the two were relieved to find themselves able to sever their business association without sacrificing their friendship.

Pennington now owned the Pen-Dike Studio (later called Pennington Studio) lock, stock, and past due bills. And Lisle packed his equipment into the Jackson wagon and prepared to pull up stakes in Durango, intending to head for Phoenix, Arizona.

To Updike's delighted surprise, at the last minute Pennington came to him and asked if he could ride along for a few miles. Pennington tied his bicycle to the back of the wagon and climbed up onto the seat beside Updike. The two rode together about twenty-five miles, talking about everything they had shared, then said an emotional good-bye.

"I was really lonely after he left," remembered Lisle, "and I wondered if I was doing the right thing. The Pennington family gave me the only real home I'd ever known . . . We'd covered many a mile together and despite our differences, we'd been good friends." But Updike was a realist and did not want to be ensnared in his old partner's debts. He picked up the reins and headed on.

Chapter

10

Lisle Updike's solitary way led him as far as St. Johns, Arizona, the seat of Apache County. A Mormon frontier town, St. Johns had pleasant homes, productive farms and ranches, prosperous businesses, and a milder climate than Durango. Lisle liked what he saw.

He asked a local tradesman if the town had a photographer. "You're looking at him," was the reply. Updike asked if it would be okay to set up shop and take some pictures. Outraged, the local photographer replied that indeed, it would not be all right and suggested that Updike go down the road and find his own town.

Undeterred, the ever-resourceful Updike got permission from the local church to use a vacant building on church property, and within a few days, he was back at work. He advertised as he had so many times before: he passed out handbills and business cards and tacked posters on buildings and fences all over town. He soon knew most of the citizens of St. Johns and became active in community affairs.

It was in St. Johns that he met and fell in love with Janet "Jenny" Jarvis. They were married on August 28, 1912, and Lisle Updike became a member of the Church of Jesus Christ of the Latter Day Saints (LDS). His studio in St. Johns prospered not only because he was a good photographer, but also because he fortunately chose a wife whose family connections assured his success in the town. He named it the Jen-Dike Studio, although it would be many months before he would change the name on the Jackson wagon.

He and Jenny made several photographic trips to Provo and Salt Lake City. He liked Utah and seriously considered moving to Salt Lake City, but the ties to St. Johns were too strong for Jenny to break, and Updike did not want to live that far from Indian Country, always his obsession as a photographer.

Remarkably, Updike left his new bride behind in St. Johns to make several trips to Durango during the first year of their marriage. Lisle had discovered that he missed Pennington more than he had foreseen, and his need to see his old friend took selfish precedence over any arrangement Jenny might have preferred.

At last, in August 1913, Lisle took Jenny with him to the mountains of Colorado for a delayed honeymoon. He wanted to show his bride some of the country where he had lived and worked prior to their marriage and to introduce her to the Penningtons. Traveling in the photo wagon, and following the old stage coach road into Hermosa Park (behind the present-day Purgatory Ski Area) and over to Rico, Lisle introduced Jenny to the spectacle of summer in high alpine country. From Rico, more steep and winding roads—and more magnificent scenery—led them down into Telluride and on to Ouray. The couple camped along the way for several days at a time, in the same places Lisle had stopped before on his solo photography trips.

This time in the mountains Updike exhibited his true artistic talent. The alpine wildflowers were in lavish bloom and the air was crisp and clean. His photographs of the rivers and streams and high meadows of the San Juan Mountains are some of the best of his career. Updike's cardinal rule for achieving strong depth of field: "focus on the foreground and stop the lens way down."

Then Jenny and Lisle crossed Red Mountain Pass on the old Otto Mears Toll Road, pausing in strategic (if precarious) locations to take photographs of the wagon on the narrow road, and drove the wagon down into Silverton. The honeymoon ended as it had begun, in Durango.

After the honeymoon trip the young Updikes spent a few days with the Penningtons before going on to Tierra Amarilla and Santa Fe. Updike's best Santa Fe photographs were taken that year, on West San Francisco Street and along the banks of the Santa Fe River. These pictures capture the charm of old Santa Fe shortly after statehood and long before it became a bustling metropolis.

Lisle and Jenny considered moving to Santa Fe but Updike "didn't think it had a future." Besides, it was too far from Jenny's hometown of St. Johns.

Updike never quite got Durango out of his mind, but St. Johns proved to be a good town for him. He became well-known and respected there and was even offered the local Ford Agency as a lure to stay in town. Selling cars, however, was neither his talent nor his desire, and he continued doing what pleased him best: roaming the countryside and taking pictures.

Still using the Jackson wagon, Updike rarely took the same route twice. Several times he crossed the San Juan River when it was nearing flood stage. "I finally figured it out. I'd ride up and down the river bank until I found a rocky spot with a nice riffle in the water. That meant the water was shallow and the bottom solid. That's where I'd cross. I got wet more than once." He also got his camera and plates wet on a crossing west of Farmington, but it was like a game to him. He liked to see if he could beat the odds. On one trip, he crossed the frozen Animas River by driving the wagon across the ice, "just to see if I could do it."

"I got used to the country, the deserts, the arroyos, and the isolation. It can be inspiring if you let it. If I had focused on the loneliness and not the adventure, I might never have been out on my own. Sometimes I'd climb a mesa and find an arrowhead or rock drawings. I liked to stand all alone on the edge of a deep canyon. Then I'd imagine that I was the first white man to ever stand at that place, and my footprints were the first white man's at that site."

Most trips in the desert country were the same in one respect: the search for water and for grass. Updike figured out that animals would gather at a water hole in the evening and leave it in the morning. One day he was desperate for water. From a viewpoint high on a mesa he had watched horses leave what appeared to be a watering hole, and he started riding toward it. "As soon as my horses smelled water, they took off. We must have been going sixty miles an hour. We came upon this muddy water hole with a band of sheep all around it. A Navajo was guarding it and his large band of sheep was taking water. The Navajo had a .30-.30 in his hands. When I came into view he hollered at me in English to get my horses out of there or he'd shoot one of them." The Navajo's wife was near the water tending a lamb. Updike told the man, "You raise that rifle and I'll kill your woman. I know how to use these six-guns. There's water enough for both of us." They eyed each other until the sheep had their fill and the Navajo moved on. Lisle kept a wary eye on the trail for the rest of the day. As he said later, "Funny how simple things like water and a few blades of grass can make a man mad enough to think about killing."

Sometimes Updike's greatest challenge was not solitude but weather. He described one particular time at a logging camp near Cortez, Colorado: "because the chemicals on the glass plates were sensitive to temperature changes, I had cleared the ground of snow, set up a tent and fired up a miner's stove. It was 40 below outside. I set one thermometer in the hypo and another in the developer on top of the stove. I let the fire go down to 70, stuck the plate in, left the tent flap up and developed by moonlight instead of a candle. I was wrapped in a sheepskin-lined coat and freezing. Then I'd put the plates in the oven to keep them warm. I was up all night making negatives. That's when I decided I'd take pictures in Colorado until winter caught up with me, then I'd head into Arizona . . ."

And sometimes the most harrowing experiences came when Updike faced a combination of elements. Robert Updike, his grandson, recalls the story of Lisle's horseback trip one cold, wet winter night, riding alone from Durango to a ranch near Mancos, about thirty miles to the west. It had been raining most of the day, but as darkness fell, the rain began to alternate with a freezing sleet. Updike realized that he still had many miles to go, and he was without tent or camping gear. It was too late to turn back to Durango, so he rode on toward the ranch. The rain and sleet continued for several hours, and when he arrived at his destination he had to ride up to the homestead's front door and shout for help. He was frozen in the saddle and could not dismount. The rancher led the horse with Updike aboard into the barn and chipped him out of the saddle with a knife.

Chapter

11

Updike did not always travel solo. Sometimes Jenny went along with him, and sometimes he shared his adventures with Penn or with his father.

Updike and Pennington reunited in 1914 at the Colorado/New Mexico Fair being held in Durango. They photographed an early Wright Model B biplane owned by the Berger Aviation Company. Harry Jackson, the former blacksmith who built Updike's special wagon, had formed this new company in association with a group of local politicians and business people. It was a dream whose time had not come.

However premature the Berger Company may have been, the Berger airplane was a great crowd pleaser. A marvel for its time but primitive by any standard, it was underpowered and could carry only the pilot and one brave passenger. Durango's 6,500 foot elevation severely impaired the plane's ability to fly. In fact, it could not even be flown to Durango; instead, it had to be disassembled and transported to the fair on the train. Even so, the plane was a thrilling sight for the citizens of Durango.

In 1915 Updike and his father drove a Model T Ford to California, where Lisle photographed the Quechan Indians. Known widely as Yumans, they were a small desert tribe, living on the California side of the Colorado River south of Yuma, Arizona. They had lived there for centuries astride the Spanish exploration routes, and had suffered gravely from disease and the white man's push for land along the fertile Colorado river delta. Through the years they had been forced onto smaller and smaller areas of land. They were historic allies of the Mohave people who lived upriver. By 1910 their best reservation land had been sold and fewer than a thousand Quechan people survived.

Updike was intrigued by the Yumans' ornate facial decorations and African-like jewelry. These Native Americans were entirely different from those he knew so well in the Four Corners area. The Yumans welcomed him and he spent several days photographing members of the tribe. Then he took a side trip to the Cocopah Reservation.

The Cocopahs, an even smaller tribe, and historic enemies of the Yuman, lived downriver. In 1915 their small reservation had not yet been set aside for their exclusive use, and they roamed freely back and forth across the Mexican border to visit tribal members living in Mexico.

The Cocopah depended on the river and the riverboat traffic for their livelihood. In 1905 American land developers had diverted the Colorado River and formed the Salton Sea. The diversion dried up the river, forcing most of the Cocopahs to disperse. (By the end of World War II the tribe numbered less than one hundred people.)

Updike found few buyers for the photographs he had taken of the poverty stricken Yuman and Cocopah Indians. These moving photos, copied from 8x10 glass plates, were rarely exhibited.

In the spring of 1918 Pennington and Updike returned to Mesa Verde. Convinced that the Jackson wagon had at last outlived its usefulness, the photographers traveled this time in a Model T Ford. Jenny came along with them, to see the famous ruins firsthand.

Apparently the Park Service had made no significant improvements to the roads since the photographers had been there in 1911. The main road to the ruins turned out to be not much better than a crude trail, presenting a fresh challenge at every turn. And it was steeper than the travelers remembered, taxing the heavily loaded Model T, whose fuel pump could not manage to get the gas into the carburetor.

Updike perched himself precariously on the running board, bracing a knee against the front fender, and with the hood open, he squirted gas from an old battery tester into the carburetor—and as he clung to the vehicle's side, Jenny took the wheel, coaxing the car up the steep grade. They lurched over ungraded and crumbling roads, occasionally stopping to move large rocks out of the way and several times pushing the car out of muddy bogs. Pennington eventually got out and walked. Remembering the trip, Updike said, "It was a lot easier when we rode horses into Mesa Verde."

In the early 1920s, Pennington wrote to Updike and asked him to come to Durango to discuss an ambitious photo project. Will Evans, a respected Shiprock, New Mexico, trader, could see that the colorful way of life of the Navajo Indians was being diluted by exposure to the white man's culture and would be gone forever within a few years. He proposed that Updike and Pennington photograph the disappearing Indian ways. It would be their last and most enduring assignment together.

Both photographers had misgivings about sharing a project again. Only when Will Evans agreed to act as guide, translator, and chief negotiator, did Updike and Pennington decide that they could accept one another as equal professionals in the undertaking.

Evans, a native of Wales, had been in the trading business for many years and knew the Navajo country and the people. Originally a coal miner, he started working in trading posts part-time; health concerns finally caused him to quit mining altogether and open his own trading post in Sanostee. It was tough going for a while, but by the time he moved from there to Shiprock in 1917, Will Evans was respected by Navajos and Anglos alike.

Updike and Pennington spent six weeks in the Shiprock area with Evans, making several trips back and forth to Durango to get supplies, process the glass plates, and make proofs. Shiprock, the rock itself, a stone monolith rising almost two thousand feet above the desert floor, provided a dramatic backdrop for many of the outdoor shots.

All of the Pennington/Updike exterior photos on this trip were taken southwest of Shiprock near the Chuska and Lukachukai Mountains or near Teec Nos Pos at the base of the Carrizo Mountains. The Navajos in the photographs lived close to Tocito Trading Post, a few miles from the old Sanostee Post and north of Two Grey Hills.

Evans's Shiprock Trading Post served as a studio for the interior shots. He furnished the rugs used in the photographs. He owned no classic Navajo wearing blankets and so the photographers had to use Navajo rugs as blanket-like garments.

It is likely that the Navajos were paid in "seco" to pose for the shots. A cash economy was practically unknown at the trading posts in Navajo country; all transactions were by trade.

Because all accounts were settled at the end of the livestock or wool season or whenever a rug was finished and offered for sale, many traders used specially made trading coins with the name of the business on each coin to help both the Indians and the trader keep track of the accounts. These coins were called "seco." There was no money and seco at least had a semblance of value.

Traders were not only merchants and livestock dealers, they also had to be pawn brokers, bankers, and advisors. Seco made it all possible. Traders also helped with the sick and injured and sometimes buried the dead, because Navajos have a strong taboo about being near dead bodies.

A trader's life was therefore a busy one and Will Evans was somewhat confined by it, but he did find short periods of time during which he could accompany the photographers and find subjects for them to photograph.

There is no record of which photographer took which individual photograph of the Navajos and the photos were never dated. Updike assigned his interests and rights to all of the Navajo photographs to Pennington but the studio continued to use the Pen-Dike name as well. The Navajo series photos were all copyrighted in Pennington's name.

Pennington advertised the Navajo series as "Early Art Photography." On the photo sheet that advertised the photographs, a third name receives credit as a Pennington photographer: W. R. Rowland. A well-known early-day Durango photographer, Rowland was also the La Plata County Surveyor and a professional engineer. His association with Pennington must have been brief; there is no further reference to him in conjunction with either Pennington or Updike.

Allan Bates, Pennington's grandson, believed that Pennington did all of the Navajo work. However, Updike said in a 1971 taped interview, "When Penn and I did the Navajo photos in the 20s, we spent weeks together."

The marked difference in technique and style among the photographs in the series is evidence of the artistic conflict between the two photographers. Updike the dramatist and Pennington the artist: theirs was a rivalry that even their enduring friendship could not overcome.

When Updike considered the Navajo project complete, he returned to St. Johns, never to collaborate again with Pennington. For a time he owned several studios in northern Arizona and as far away as Provo, Utah, but eventually he concentrated his energy on a chain of Updike Studios in Phoenix.

Pennington continued to travel and photograph the Native Americans with further help from Will Evans. In 1926 they traveled together over terrain new to Evans—over the Lukachukai Mountains, into the Chinle Valley, and on to the Hopi Mesas, accompanied by John Stewart MacClary, a writer from Pueblo, Colorado, and MacClary's brother. The group spent several days at Hopi, exploring and photographing several villages.

Chapter

12

One of the most interesting subjects in the Navajo series is the old medicine man and warrior, Bi-Joshii. Pennington photographed him at Evans Trading Post and again as the old man emerged from a "guest" hogan at Sanostee Trading Post. (The hogan was available for Navajo families who might find themselves stranded for the night at the store.)

Bi-Joshii, a survivor of the Navajo Long Walk in 1864–68, was a strong-minded leader who deeply resented American domination of Navajo land and people. He had suffered through the years in Fort Sumner and had little use for the U.S. Government or its laws. When he returned to the Southwest, Bi-Joshii built his home high on the slopes of Beautiful Mountain directly west of Sanostee, wishing to have little contact with the Americans.

But Bi-Joshii was not to be left in peace. William T. Shelton, the Indian Department Superintendent at Shiprock, angered Bi-Joshii and other Navajos by enforcing a ban against plural marriages. Shelton was a hard man to reason with. To back up his ban Shelton ordered the capture of several men, including two sons of old Bi-Joshii. The Navajos were rounded up, along with their wives, and locked up in the Shiprock jail.

The infuriated Bi-Joshii launched an attack against the jail while Shelton was away from his office. After severely beating one of Shelton's men, the Indians succeeded in springing the prisoners. Recruiting volunteers along the way, Bi-Joshii fled with his renegade band back to Beautiful Mountain, where the rebels set up a strong defensive position. This action is known as the Beautiful Mountain Rebellion and was the last serious resistance by American Indians to U.S. authority.

Most Anglos took the threat seriously. They knew Bi-Joshii and his hatred of Shelton and so wanted to stay clear of the old man. Red Rock Trading Post north of Sanostee was closed and evacuated, as was the Bureau of Indian Affairs sawmill south of Bi-Joshii's stronghold.

It was a tense time. Both sides refused to negotiate a settlement. After a stand-off of several months a detachment of more than 200 troops from the 12th Cavalry, Ft. Robinson, Nebraska, arrived by train in Gallup and proceeded to Shiprock to quell the uprising.

By this time, press reports had blown the importance of the incident out of proportion. And Shelton, who probably could have settled the issue by negotiation, chose instead to pursue the Navajos into the mountains. Many people expected a full-fledged bloodbath.

The entire affair lasted several months. A series of conferences were held at the Sanostee store. Apparently aware of Shelton's role in escalating the conflict, his superiors ordered him not to attend. Shelton was irate and railed against the Army, his superiors, and Bi-Joshii, but the orders remained in effect and he stayed away from the meetings. Bi-Joshii and his sons were persuaded to surrender, after which they were moved to Gallup and on to Santa Fe for their trial. The renegades were sentenced to serve token jail time. Not a shot had been fired.

One way or another Shelton was determined to punish any person whom he suspected of leaning toward Bi-Joshii. He turned his wrath on the Noel family, owners of the trading post at Sanostee, and Bi-Joshii sympathizers. Shelton authorized that another trading post permit be issued for Tocito, only a few miles away. The Tocito store cut deeply into Sanostee's trade. Perhaps this satisfied Shelton's need for revenge.

Will Evans's son, Dave, says that old Bi-Joshii was known as "Link," referring to the "missing link" because of his appearance. His sons, medicine men in their own right, were known as "Big Link" and "Little Link"; Bi-Joshii's band of Navajos was the "Link Gang." Dave Evans recalls Bi-Joshii riding his horse into Shiprock and trading at his father's store. "He'd threaten us with his riding stick."

Esenapa Martin, a Navajo woman, was living with her family near Beautiful Mountain at the time of the Rebellion. She recalled the terror old Bi-Joshii, actually her uncle, inflicted on her father and family members when he rode into their camp demanding that all the men follow him up on the Mountain. "Shelton's men were close behind and my father was able to run and hide. We were terrified of Bi-Joshii. He was an evil man with great power. People made fun of him behind his back and called him 'the missing link' but there was something truly sinister about Bi-Joshii."

Old age and failing health finally forced Bi-Joshii to give up his warlike ways. He remained until his death at home on Beautiful Mountain, still bitter from his defeat and humiliation by Shelton's men.

Esenapa Martin died in 1988 at the age of ninety-seven. In the late 1970s she identified most of the subjects and locales in the Updike/Pennington Navajo series. Affectionately known as "Grandma" Martin by family and friends alike, she lived out her days in a small rock house near the Hogback, not far from Shiprock.

Chapter

13

The Great Depression struck the country not many years after Pennington and Updike completed the Navajo series. Durango had its share of tough times and widespread unemployment. The American Smelting and Refining Company closed the Durango smelter in the early 1930s, the railroads were all in receivership, and many bankrupt small businesses left gaping holes and empty storefronts up and down Durango's Main Avenue. Miners, railroaders, farmers, ranchers, sawmillers—hundreds were out of work. Little money was in circulation.

Yet Pennington survived. There was a steady demand for family portraits and other photographs. Like other merchants he frequently received payment for his work in the form of a bushel of potatoes, a ham, a chicken, a sack of coal, or maybe an I.O.U. He managed to acquire the building that housed his studio, as well as his family's apartment and several others.

One of the highlights of this otherwise bleak time in Durango was a local marvel known as "Moving Mountain," which Pennington considered a fair photographic subject. In the early 1930s, a coal mine fire and the subsequent collapse of the mine created this phenomenon as the mountain slipped downward on a natural fault. Rocks, boulders, trees, and dirt cascaded down the steep slope. It became one of Durango's greatest attractions for locals and tourists alike. Walter Winchell, famed columnist, falsely reported in a Sunday night broadcast in 1934 that Moving Mountain had dammed off the Animas River and the entire population of Durango had been moved to high ground. (Durango's Bodo Business Park and the Durango Mall now occupy most of the land near Moving Mountain.)

Most people who knew Pennington say that he was a quiet and thoughtful man who was active in community affairs and in his church and was never too busy to talk to an interested youngster. Others say that in his later years, as his health began to fail and financial conditions worsened, he became short-tempered, cross, and moody.

In 1936 Frank Stepleton arrived in Durango from Lima, Ohio. Pennington hired him, sight unseen, in response to an ad Stepleton had placed in a Denver newspaper. Stepleton, a superb photographer in his own right, rode buses, passenger trains, and the narrow gauge railroad in his determination to get to Durango, and Pennington immediately put him to work. Within a few months, Penn made Stepleton manager of a new shop, a small auxiliary studio in the lobby of the old Gem Theater at 1001 Main Avenue, a block up the street from the main studio.

According to Stepleton, the separate studio arrangement was an attempt to drive a competitor out of town. Fishback Studio, located a few doors north of the Gem, was a family photography outfit specializing in family and school class photos, and offered no real competition to Pennington's carefully planned studio work. But during the Depression every dime counted, and Fishback was doing a good business that Pennington wanted for himself. In the branch studio, Stepleton had a 5x7 camera, a darkroom, and some photo props. He specialized in "three for a dime quick photos," and referred any serious portrait work to Pennington. But the ploy to grab Fishback's share of the market did not work. Fishback Studio continued attracting the customers they always had and remained in operation for many years.

Stepleton said that Pennington, who never seemed to feel well, was a difficult and demanding boss who failed to appreciate the work of his employees, and was, in Stepleton's word, "henpecked." Rose Pennington put impossible demands on her husband both for money and for time. Stepleton recalls that she summoned her husband by shouting into the heating duct directly over the studio. Pennington would drop whatever he was doing and rush upstairs to heed her call.

Magazine articles written in the 1930s and '40s featured either Pennington or Updike but never both together. Pennington rarely acknowledged Updike in interviews; Updike seldom mentioned Pennington by name.

John Stewart MacClary, in a series in *Desert Magazine* in 1937–1939, wrote more than a score of articles without mentioning Updike once; Pennington got all of the credit. Diane Thomas wrote a comprehensive article about Updike for *True West Magazine* in 1976 and referred to Pennington not by name, but only as "Updike's partner" or his "old buddy from Texas."

In 1938 Pennington suffered a heart attack and moved to Arizona. He left Stepleton in charge of the Durango studio, paying him less than twenty dollars a week. With no future as a Pennington employee and insufficient money to buy the business outright, Stepleton set about making plans to leave Durango. Meanwhile, Pennington's building and apartments were foreclosed by the bank. Just in time, Dr. J. B. Ochsner, a local physician and himself a prize-winning photographer, loaned Stepleton the money to buy out his absent boss, including the respected Pennington trademark. After serving in World War II, Stepleton returned to Durango to build a new place for his expanded Pennington Studio and Camera Shop. Under yet again another owner, the business still bears the Pennington name today.

Although Pennington had left Durango for Arizona and eventually California, he and Updike remained in contact, their professional differences apparently set aside in favor of cordial relations. And when William Pennington died in 1940, his old friend and occasional rival Lisle Updike was at his side.

By the 1930s Lisle Updike's principal business was in Phoenix, but he kept close ties to the Southwest and returned frequently to his vacation home in Durango. He loved to "go jeeping," delighted as always to travel on unmaintained mountain roads no matter how perilous, and often treated his passengers to breath-catching views of the high country from the very spots where he had set up his camera years before. Jenny Updike died in 1944, and Lisle remarried in 1946. He and his new bride, Ethel Speare, traveled together almost as frequently in their retirement as the photographer had in his early life. He had found a companion to share in his wanderlust.

Updike Studios remain in operation in Phoenix, Arizona, under corporate ownership. Lisle Updike died in 1976.

Today, nearly a century after Pennington and Updike first met, we are richer for the legacy of their outstanding work. Their unforgettable images preserve for us lost aspects of Southwestern life, seen through the lens of earlier times so different from our own. And in their exceptional photographs of American Indians, we see not only a vanished way of tribal life, we also recognize the deep and genuine respect the photographers felt for every one of their subjects. When we study this great body of their work, we come to appreciate the allure those wagon-rutted roads held for William Marion Pennington and Lisle Chandler Updike.

Zuni, May 1909

17 PLATES

Towa Yal'lanne, Corn Mountain, Sacred Place of the Zuni, from rooftop in Zuni Pueblo. Updike: "I'd been to the top of that mountain during the Shalako ceremonies in 1901."

Updike: "This is my favorite photo. It shows our wagon on the left with our photographic tent poles hanging out the back. The other wagon is Jim Slade's. We'd stopped at a place called Chinaman's Springs about halfway to Gallup from Farmington. We were all getting along fine by this time. Penn is fixing biscuits on the tailgate of our wagon. I'm kneeling on the ground. Slade is on the left next to Mrs. Slade and Mr. Holgate is on the right."

Bridge and Horno at Zuni. Pennington and Updike camped a few hundred yards back from this bridge. The surprisingly sophisticated bridge across the Zuni River was made of logs and timbers and stood on stone pilings in the water. The river is dry in summer but can become a raging torrent during spring rains. The beehive-like structure is a bread oven or *horno*, introduced into the Southwest by the Spanish in the 16th century. It is made of adobe bricks or stone. Fires are built of juniper wood at night and the oven is sealed off except for an air hole in the top. In the morning most of the ashes are scraped out and the bread is placed in the horno and baked by the retained heat in the walls. The bread is prepared in the homes in large pottery dough bowls.

Checkerboard garden plots at Zuni. A light dusting of snow remains on the ground from the previous night's storm. Water is a precious commodity in Zuni. In order to conserve it, the Zunis used small square garden plots, lined them with clay, then brought in fertile soil for planting. The growing plots were easily weeded and watered. Women carried water to the plots in pottery jugs or *ollas* balanced on their heads. A vertical coyote fence and an adobe wall discourage animals from entering the garden area.

Small Zuni Plaza. Updike: "Many of the Zuni homes could only be entered by first climbing up a ladder to a rooftop and then down into a plaza where there were doors."

Zuni man in a special work area designed for artisans is drilling turquoise with a pump drill. A pump drill consists of a round rod with a metal point or drill fastened to its end. A wooden crossbar is linked to the rod by leather thongs. The thongs are wound around the rod. When the crossbar is pressed down, the rod rotates. A skilled artisan can keep it going consistently by applying the right pressure.

A Zuni man drilling turquoise with a pump drill as neighbors look on. Note tailormade work place with a seat, foot rest and support for drilling surface. The man wears hand stitched pants and a headband. He also wears several strands of turquoise nuggets that he probably drilled.

Zuni women grinding cornmeal. Updike: "This is women's work. Every woman in the village came here to grind her corn." Coarsely ground corn is in the basket on the left. The middle basket contains partially ground, and the fine finished flour is in the right hand basket. The Anasazi ground their corn on stone slabs known as metates and used a stone *mano*, or grinding tool. The bits of stone which were inevitably ground into the flour caused great damage to the teeth. These women use wooden grinding surfaces and a stone mano to eliminate much of the grit.

Zuni woman preparing to grind cornmeal.

Updike: "He was cutting and sewing tanned buckskin into moccasins." Buckskin is highly prized for moccasins and leggings. It is tanned with the brain of the animal, usually deer, and is relatively waterproof. The man wears a pair of handmade moccasins.

"If the Navajo learned to weave from the Zunis, as many believe, then William Pennington photographed an ancient art being practiced in 1909," John Stewart MacClary, writing in *Desert Magazine,* 1936. The loom, which has no frame, is an adaptation of a back-strap loom. The weaver wears a coarse cotton shawl, a dress of block print store-bought calico. She is using prespun Germantown yarn in her rug, which she is weaving on a foundation of cotton warp. No weaving is done in Zuni today.

Zuni Kachina carver. Cottonwood used in carving is scarce in Zuni. A pile of small driftwood pieces are alongside the carver. Kachina carving is still practiced, but not as extensively as in Hopi.

Updike: "The women made large pieces of fine pottery that they called *ollas*. They carried grain and other foods with pots balanced on their heads." Zuni is primarily a pueblo of jewelry makers. There are few practicing Zuni potters.

Zuni woman with pot.

Pennington: Old Mission Church, "Our Lady of Guadalupe," first constructed in 1929, destroyed in the 1680 Pueblo Revolt, and rebuilt in 1699. When Pennington took this photo the mission was little more than a ruin, but now is almost completely restored. It is under the jurisdiction of St. Anthony's Mission to the Zuni.

Many of the Zuni women wore elaborate hand woven *mantas*, or shawls, but some, as this woman, had store-bought shawls.

The child in this photograph was unaffected by having his picture taken, despite the Zuni's fear that the camera might "steal his soul."

Acoma, May 1909

4 PLATES

San Estevan del Rey, the old Spanish Mission at Acoma Pueblo, built between 1630 and 1645 by Franciscan Father Ramirez. Updike: "Penn and I'd seen a photo by William H. Jackson of this same mission taken several years earlier, and we placed our cameras in almost the same spot." Between the time of Jackson's photo and Updike's, new adobe had been added to the towers, and the entire building had been repaired and stabilized.

An Acoma mother and two children return home after mass at San Estevan Mission.

A potter poses at doorway of her home in the Sky City. Women wear dresses of store bought cloth and woolen blankets or mantas. Acoma had become a prime producer of large pottery which was decorated using native pigments, painted freehand in intricate patterns.

Potters in the Sky City.

Jicarilla Apache, 1909

12 PLATES

A Jicarilla Apache maiden, Dulce, New Mexico.

Jicarilla Apache with eagle feather headdress.

Jicarilla Apache with eagle feather headdress.

Jicarilla Apaches.

Jicarilla Apaches.

Jicarilla Apaches.

Jicarilla Apache.

Jicarilla Apaches.

Jicarilla Apache.

Jicarilla Apache.

Jicarilla Apache.

Jicarilla Apache.

144

Ute

3 PLATES

Buckskin Charley, photographed wearing Peace Medal in 1910 or 1912 by Updike.

Buckskin Charley, photographed by Updike about 1930. Buckskin Charley
died in May 1936, at the age of 95.

Land Rush Day, Ignacio, Colorado, approximately 1912. After the Utes gave up their claim to certain tribal lands, these lands were offered to white settlers on a first come basis. In the left foreground of the photo, Updike's photo wagon can be seen with tent erected.

Yuma Indians, 1915 or 1916

19 PLATES

Yuma, Arizona. Jumbo and his wife.

George Updike posing by Yuma Indian home.

Yuma mother with child in cradle board.

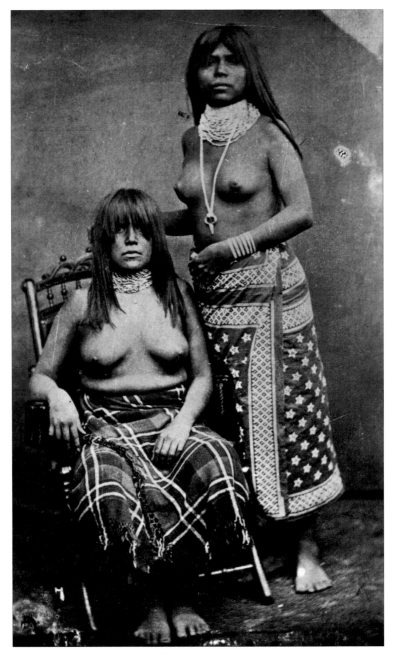

Updike: "In order to avoid the desert heat, some of the younger women stripped to the waist and spent the day in the shade of the home or summer shelters."

Updike: "All the Yuma people were friendly, but very shy."

Yuma Indian.

Yuma Indian.

Yuma Indians.

Yuma Indians.

Yuma Indian.

Yuma Indian.

Yuma Indians.

Yuma Indians.

Yuma Indian.

Yuma Indian.

Yuma Indian.

Yuma Indian.

Yuma Indian.

Yuma Indians.

The Navajo Series

24 PLATES

Advertising photo montage. To advertise his line of Navajo Series Photos, William Pennington printed an advertising photo with a brief description of each image. Although Updike was no longer a partner in the business, the "Pen-Dike" name was used. In the corner of each photo, Pennington used his name and the word "Navajo." W. R. Rowland is given credit as a proprietor.

Relating an Experience. Taken on a mesa near Teec Nos Pos, Arizona. Trader Will Evans said, "the Navajo is a natural born storyteller. The storyteller has the ear of the listener without interruption until the story is fully told, and then the teller becomes the listener in turn, and an exchange of news is made." Sleeping Ute Mountain and the cities of Mesa Verde can be seen in the distance.

Indian Madonna. Will Evans captioned a personal copy of this print: "The pride and joy of the Navajo people is their children. In sickness or in health nothing within the means of the parents is too good for them. Well-to-do families have been known to impoverish themselves in the hiring of medicine men for the healing of their sick children."

Silversmith at Work. Unknown silversmith fashions conchas for a belt. Photo was the model for a bronze by Durango Artist Clyde Doney in 1978.

Near the Base of Shiprock. Shiprock stands alone in the desert a few miles south of the town of Shiprock. Rising nearly 2,000 feet above the desert floor, it can be seen for miles and at a certain time in the year will cast a shadow on the cliffs of the Mesa Verde fifty miles to the northeast.

In the Glow of the Campfire. One of Pennington's favorite poses. Will Evans said, "the simple dignity of this old man tells a story of himself and his people, proud of themselves and their culture, and strong enough to withstand the changes of time."

Ready for the Enemy. Bi-Joshii, the aged Navajo Medicine man and warrior emerges from the guest hogan near Sanostee Trading Post. Bi-Joshii in 1913 led the Beautiful Mountain Rebellion against American authority. A strong leader and defiant foe of Indian Superintendent Agency W. T. Shelton, he posed for this Pennington photo in the early 1920s.

Indian Baby Carriage. The baby's grandmother has secured him in the traditional Navajo cradle board where he would remain most of the day. Esenapa "Grandma" Martin, a highly respected Navajo elder, in 1978 identified the lady as "Hosteen Joe's number two wife." Mrs. Martin knew many of the people in the Navajo series.

The Watchman. From high on a mesa near Teec Nos Pos a Navajo tribes-
man recreates the role of the watchman ever vigilant for approaching
enemies.

A Navajo Gentleman. One of Pennington's most popular images in the Navajo series. "Grandma" Martin remembered him as Hosteen Joe, a neighbor from Sanostee, Arizona.

An Indian Maid With Her Flock. Hosteen Joe's number one wife tends her band near her hogan at Sanostee. Note the obvious presence of "Old Navajo Sheep" or Churros in the band. They are distinctive with the long straight wool that is highly prized by Navajo weavers. The churros are descended from animals brought to the New World by the Spanish. They were almost wiped out in the stock reduction programs of the 1930s and have only recently been reintroduced into Navajoland.

Navajo Weavers. Three women weaving on two rugs near the hogan of Hosteen Joe by Sanostee. The infant is in the cradle board for safe keeping while the women weave.

Directing the Messenger. An obvious pose in an attempt to recreate the old days. The Navajo rugs being used as blankets are Teec Nos Pos designs from the stock at Will Evans's Shiprock Trading Post.

Solid Comfort. Hosteen Joe's daughter and granddaughter. One of Pennington's favorite Navajo portraits.

An Old Warrior. The old warrior and medicine man Bi-Joshii.

A Strong Character. Hatali Yazzie (Little Singer or Healer), Bi-Joshii's oldest son and a co-conspirator in the Beautiful Mountain Rebellion. Like his father, defiant until his death.

190

An Indian Judge. Judge Klah, Judge or Justice of the Peace in Shiprock. Grandma Martin said, "Everybody liked Judge Klah. He was related to Hosteen Klah, the medicine man from Newcomb."

Parting Friends. Two old friends say goodbye. They shake hands in the Navajo way—by barely touching the hand of the other person. No hearty handshakes in the Navajo culture.

*Judge Claw [sic] and his two wive*s. Plural marriages were common until the 1920s. Apparently Judge Klah lived openly with great respect from his Navajo people.

Home. Hosteen Joe's Hogan near Sanostee with his two wives and family. The style of hogan construction is "forked stick." The basic design is around forked sticks arranged like a tee-pee and then filled with earth, brush, and smaller logs. It is very rare. Few survive today.

A Noted Medicine Man. Will Evans: "Hosteen Bedugai, Mr. Mustache of the Hosclishni Clan. Brother of Shaky Hand, Shorty Nez, and Hosh Clishni Nez. He worked for many years at Hogback Trading Company for Wilford Wheeler."

Toh-Atin Trading Co. 13. The Weaver. This photo was not included in the original Pennington montage, but became a very popular image. Will Evans: "This is the ancient swastika design. Weaver's clothing is typical: multiple skirts of calico or sateen; blouse of velveteen. Airholes are provided at the armpits to give ventilation. Pennington took this photo in 1930."

The Cocopa

2 PLATES

Cocopa man near Yuma, 1915 or 1916.

Cocopa family dwelling.